IRAN
Architecture for Changing Societies

An international seminar co-sponsored by the

Tehran Museum of Contemporary Art
Iranian Cultural Heritage Organisation
Iranian Ministry of Housing and Urban Development
Aga Khan Award for Architecture

11-17 October 2002, Yazd and Tehran, Iran

EDITED BY PHILIP JODIDIO

UMBERTO ALLEMANDI & C.
for

Aga Khan Award for Architecture

Front cover
The dome of Masjid Jami', Yazd, Iran, 14th century

Back cover
Kamran Diba, Tehran Museum of Contemporary Art, Tehran, Iran, 1976

Preface

LUÌS MONREAL, GENERAL MANAGER
AGA KHAN TRUST FOR CULTURE, GENEVA, SWITZERLAND

The Aga Khan Trust for Culture (AKTC) and the Aga Khan Award for Architecture (AKAA) had been considering for some time the organisation of a meeting in Iran that would provide the opportunity of engaging in meaningful dialogue between national architects, teachers and students in the fields of historic preservation and contemporary design, and their counterparts from other countries. This initiative was realised in the cities of Yazd and Tehran from 11 to 17 October 2002.

The seminars organised by the Trust and the Award for Architecture have contributed to setting high academic and professional standards for nearly three decades, and complement the educational activities undertaken by other agencies of the Aga Khan Development Network (AKDN). The meetings in Iran, however, marked the first time that an Award seminar has been split into two different but complementary subjects: historic preservation and contemporary architecture and planning. This dual structure closely reflects the realities that most Muslim societies face today. On one hand, there is an urgent need to protect and revitalise historic urban heritage and the contexts in which it is located; on the other, there is massive need for new construction, including housing, industrial and corporate structures, public facilities, and planning and infrastructure initiatives. Unfortunately, most countries separate these concerns. The AKTC, however, follows an integrated approach to the challenge of reconciling the old with the new, and conceives of the past as an integral part of contemporary life. Thus, the Trust believes that the union of preservation of heritage with contemporary initiatives is a necessary prerequisite for the attainment of truly sustainable development.

The two themes of the seminar were mirrored in the venues where the meetings were held. Few cities in the world can rival the extraordinary architectural heritage of Yazd, and Tehran is a fine example of a modern metropolis, filled with energy and excitement, but also with many of the same problems of burgeoning cities everywhere. The striking contrast between the two provided vivid illustration for the seminar sessions, while one constant and very enjoyable characteristic of both cities was the kind friendship and warm hospitality extended to us by the Iranian men and women who so graciously welcomed our presence.

It has been an honour for the Trust that the seminar was organised under the auspices and with the close collaboration of the Iranian Cultural Heritage Organisation, the Iranian Ministry of Housing and Urban Development and the Tehran Museum of Contemporary Art. The professional relations and warm personal friendships that we have established with all three organisations are indeed most important to us, and we look forward to nurturing these relationships in the future.

I would like to thank particularly Mr Seyyed Mohammad Beheshti, Head of the Iranian Cultural Heritage Organisation (ICHO), as well as the members of the ICHO staff. Mr Mohammad Hassan Khademzadeh, Director of the ICHO in Yazd, and his colleagues were also most helpful. We are grateful to Dr Mohammad Ali Vahdat, Chancellor of the University of Yazd, who made available the university's Cultural Centre in Yazd as the venue for our meetings there. I also wish to thank Dr Pirooz Hanachi, Deputy Minister of Housing and Urban Development, for his constant support and assistance. Dr Ali Reza Sami Azar, Director of the Tehran Museum of Contemporary Art, and his staff hosted the sessions in Tehran, and provided invaluable assistance for the administrative and logistical organisation of our meetings. During Dr Sami Azar's mandate, the Tehran Museum of Contemporary Art has become the most important cultural venue in Iran, open to academics, professionals and most importantly to students, thousands of whom attended the seminar sessions in Tehran.

Finally, I would like to extend my special thanks to Dr Bagher Shirazi who helped to conceive the intellectual programme for the seminar sessions held in Yazd, and to Professor Darab Diba who helped to plan the entire seminar from its inception through to the end.

These proceedings of our meetings will help to convey a sense of the extremely rich exchange and breadth of ideas that were discussed in Yazd and Tehran. The Aga Khan Trust for Culture and the Aga Khan Award for Architecture are proud to have been part of this event and hope to long continue the fruitful relations established at numerous levels of Iranian society.

Preface

PIROOZ HANACHI, DEPUTY MINISTER
MINISTRY OF HOUSING AND URBAN DEVELOPMENT, TEHRAN, IRAN

I would like to thank our co-organisers at the Tehran Museum of Contemporary Art and to welcome all our guests. I hope that holding such seminars may provide the grounds for an exchange of views between Iranian architects and international personalities worldwide.

I found several interesting points in the lecture given by Charles Jencks, who outlined seven phases in the generation of new ideas in architecture. He also discussed the interactive relationship between globalisation and architecture. When we look at the world's contemporary history, we see that architecture, unlike language, has never bound itself to conventional borders. The evidence of this fact is detectable throughout the world over a period of centuries. Today, architects can take advantage of information systems to have immediate access to new ideas. The accelerating effect that these information systems have on architectural ideas is undeniable.

Obviously, the effect of globalisation on different fields of architecture will be discussed in this seminar. Globalisation has merged the work place into the living environment and exerts a great influence on the ideas we have encountered in previous decades. Today, virtual shopping means that sales can occur without stores in the physical sense. This will obviously affect the real environment.

There were three pivotal points in Professor Jencks' remarks. He believes that inspiration by nature, inspiration by environment, and the emergence of a certain spirit of the times are key elements in the most important works of architecture at the beginning of the third millennium. When we look at the history of Iran's architecture, which has always been distinctive in the Middle East, we see that it contains these three elements.

Iranian architecture in the pre-Islamic period was based on conformity with the environment and introverted creation within a certain spirit of the times, whereas western architecture demonstrated these characteristics in an extroverted manner. One distinction between eastern and western architecture is perhaps that of introversion versus extroversion, a difference that demands careful consideration.

I hope that this seminar, which was coordinated by concerned Iranian organisers and an international institution, will occur again in the future. My special thanks go to the Aga Khan Award for Architecture. The exchange of ideas here will definitely have a great influence on Iranian architects, students, and all those who are involved in this profession. A major source of concern in Iran is that we have not developed any new ideas in architecture for a long time and we hope that this seminar will provide the grounds for generating such new thought.

Although positive steps have been taken in this regard, the government's inadequacy in creating new ideas in architecture prevails. Of course, providing a fertile ground for future development is our job and we hope that your cooperation will help us to succeed.

Preface

ALI REZA SAMI AZAR, DIRECTOR
TEHRAN MUSEUM OF CONTEMPORARY ART, TEHRAN, IRAN

It is an honour for the Tehran Museum of Contemporary Art to host such a group of prominent international architects and urban designers. This is a unique opportunity for Iranian architects to take advantage of dialogue and discourse on major issues facing contemporary architecture. It will surely enhance our knowledge and increase our ability to tackle current problems confronting physical necessities of our changing society. This seminar was presented in two parts. The first part, held in the city of Yazd, looked at ways and means for maintaining historical heritage and renovating existing sites and buildings. The second part, held in this museum, focussed on trends in contemporary architecture, searching for appropriate alternatives for the future. It thus had a two-fold agenda looking at how to preserve the architectural achievements of the past while at the same time confronting the new necessities of the modern world.

These two areas, that of a traditional heritage arising from an old civilisation and the requirements of today's world, do not seem to be able to coexist easily. There are contradictions that sometimes give rise to disagreements. The progressive ambitions of mankind may unfortunately tend towards the elimination of traditional institutions and cultural resources. At the same time, there is a growing fear that this so-called single-world culture is a force that is progressively wearing away the cultural heritage that made the great civilisations of the past.

This clash is complex in a country such as Iran where there is a strong cultural background as well as a vigorous tendency towards progress and a thirst for modernity. The emergence of new architecture in Iran was of course related to the wave of modernity that has tended to impose a certain global conformity. Some of the buildings erected during the past few decades however, including this museum, exemplify the strong desire of leading Iranian architects to root contemporary architecture in the soil of its past and to infuse a national spirit in their works, while travelling the road towards modernisation. A quick glance at the city of Tehran indicates that there have been only isolated attempts in this direction.

The crucial problem confronting nations is one of underdevelopment. But is there any universal solution to this problem? The phenomenon of globalisation, truly considered an advancement of mankind, simultaneously constitutes a subtle destruction of traditional cultures and national values. This could eventually mean the complete subversion of great civilisations and old cultures. These civilisations and cultures permit us to interpret life and define the ethical and mythical nucleus of mankind. The paradoxical question is therefore how to become modern while also returning to our roots; how to preserve an old civilisation and to simultaneously be part of universal culture. This dilemma proves the growing need for an authentic dialogue, an exchange of ideas and a sharing of experiences. This seminar intends to provide the grounds for precisely that kind of dialogue. It will hopefully familiarise Iranians with the architectural initiatives of other nations, as we can no longer apply old solutions to new problems. It will also explain how Iranian contemporary architects have dealt with new necessities and modern physical requirements.

This gathering fulfils a long-awaited wish. I am deeply grateful to everyone who has been involved in the realisation of this wish. Firstly, I would like to express my deepest appreciation to our Iranian co-organisers, the Iranian Cultural Heritage Organisation, and above all to Mr Beheshti, and also to the Iranian Ministry of Housing and Urban Development represented by Dr Hanachi, Deputy Minister. My heartfelt gratitude goes to our friends at the Aga Khan Trust for Culture and the Aga Khan Award for Architecture. In this regard, I must single out for special thanks Dr Suha Özkan, without whose full-fledged collaboration and dedication the organisation of this seminar would not have been possible. I am also equally grateful to Mr Farrokh Derakhshani, who has been shuttling to and fro between Geneva and Tehran to coordinate all the concerned parties. Ladies and gentlemen, let us hope that this auspicious gathering will bring about more determination and insight to building a better environment for a new society.

Introduction. Past and Future

PHILIP JODIDIO

It is a commonplace notion that the worlds of contemporary architecture and historic preservation rarely meet. Architects, especially famous ones, are so much involved in the present that they hardly have time for the past. And the issues of historic preservation, including the technical ones, are very different from the questions posed by a modern computer-designed building for example. And yet, what are great cities but a continual confrontation between the needs of these two disciplines. History is defined in different ways in Paris, Cairo or New York, but each city has its past, its monuments and its heritage that largely define its identity. Moving forward to accommodate new populations or new activities frequently gives rise to conflict between past and present. Is a monument more important than a new high-rise that creates office space or apartments for the populations of today? It may be that architects and specialists in historic preservation have very different points of view on such a problem. And yet it would appear that a greater sensitivity to the past exists in more mature western cities that may no longer be growing as rapidly as cities such as Tehran for example. Why bring together contemporary architects and important figures in the world of historic preservation in the same seminar? Because it is urgent that a dialogue be created and that students who listen to their words be familiar not only with the alluring prospect of shining new buildings, but also with the wealth that lies in the stones of the past.

Participants in the seminar co-organised by the Aga Khan Award for Architecture in Yazd and Tehran have themselves actively posed the questions of the relationship between the past, the present and the future implied in such a gathering. As Seyyed Mohammad Beheshti, Head of the Iranian Cultural Heritage Organisation, puts it: "It is undoubtedly laudable to strive towards a better future and to pay attention to the past as an indispensable factor in achieving this future. However, this idea should not conceal a greater truth from us: the past and the future do not exist; what does exist is the present. [...] It is correct that the demolition of the past by the relentless forces of modernity is quite disturbing, but it is also important to understand the reasons for its preservation, as well as its employment for the benefit in the present. If we clearly comprehend the benefits of the past and if we understand its advantages for our present, then it will be preserved and delivered to the future as it should be."

The architecture of the present is surely the product of past lessons, even if some schools of thought such as early Modernism imagined history as a *tabula rasa*. Arata Isozaki, one of the most important living Japanese architects, a participant in this seminar, in describing his own career, says: "...I started studying not only modern architecture but also the history of architecture – traditional Japanese architecture, but also that of Europe. I came to understand the solutions found in different parts of the world in the past and to begin to see relations between these methods. I became determined not to simply follow a modern style, but by enriching my thoughts with the learning of the past, I sought to create something new." Isozaki is in reality no exception to the rule. Great contemporary architects must look to what has gone before in order to be able to go forward, "to create something new," as he puts it. If the great examples of past architecture, as exemplified in many historic city cores, are allowed to be swept aside by modernisation, then clearly tomorrow's architects will have little to base their thought on.

Where architectural education once placed great emphasis on learning such antiquated methods as drawing, today, computers and a hurried sense of the future often sweep aside the kind of historical thought that nourished the work of Arata Isozaki. As Seyyed Mohammad Beheshti, Luìs Monreal and other participants in this seminar have underlined, the most significant moment for both historic preservation and contemporary architecture is not the future but the present. The present is also where the past and the future meet. Whether in rehabilitating time-worn relics or in imagining glittering new vessels, specialists in historic preservation and in contemporary architecture have every interest in getting to know each other better. It is their combined effort that shapes the city of today.

Contents

CHALLENGES FOR IRAN

FARROKH DERAKHSHANI
17   Iran and the Aga Khan Award for Architecture

SEYYED MOHAMMAD BEHESHTI
21   The Art of Revitalisation

MOHAMMAD HASSAN KHADEMZADEH
27   Continuity and Change in the City of Yazd

DARAB DIBA AND MOZAYAN DEHBASHI
31   Trends in Modern Iranian Architecture

S. HADI MIRMIRAN
39   Public Buildings in Iran: 1920 to the Present

RESTORING THE CITY: BUILDING ANEW

SHADIA TOUQAN
61   Revitalise to Survive: the Old City of Jerusalem

SÉMIA AKROUT-YAÏCHE
65   New Life for the Medina of Tunis

NASSIM SHARIPOV AND SELMA AL-RADI
69   The Heritage of Bukhara

NADER ARDALAN
75   Building in the Persian Gulf

AYDAN BALAMIR
83   Turkey Between East and West

NEW PERSPECTIVES: THE AGA KHAN TRUST FOR CULTURE

STEFANO BIANCA
111   Urban Conservation in the Islamic World

RENATA HOLOD
119   Our Works Point to Us: Restoration and the Award

Contents (continued)

SUHA ÖZKAN
125   Appreciating High Technology

PETER DAVEY
131   Celebrating Islamic Tradition: Looking Ahead

ANSWERS FOR THE FUTURE

CHARLES JENCKS
155   The New Paradigm in Architecture

ARATA ISOZAKI
163   The Virtues of Modernity

PHILIP JODIDIO
167   Architecture Now!

KEN YEANG
177   Eco-Design and Planning

MICHAEL SORKIN
183   Eleven Tasks for Urban Design

RODO TISNADO
189   The Technology of Perfection

BABAR KHAN MUMTAZ
193   Epilogue

215   APPENDIX: LIST OF PARTICIPANTS

CHALLENGES FOR IRAN

Iran and the Aga Khan Award for Architecture

FARROKH DERAKHSHANI

When the Aga Khan Award for Architecture was founded in 1977, the architecture of Iran was going through a period of rapid change, as was the case with many other Muslim societies. However, it had come to be better known in the international architectural arena due to a number of important events which took place there. The two International Congresses of Architects held in Shiraz in 1970 and Isfahan in 1974 brought some of the world's most important architects and urban planners of the time to Iran, introducing them to the contemporary practice in the country as well as giving an opportunity to Iranian architects to have direct contact with these figures. In 1976, the first International Congress of Women Architects was also held in Iran. Another important factor was the staging of an international competition for the National Library in 1977, which drew what was at the time a record number of international and national entries. Following these events, a number of these architects were also invited to build projects in Iran, including Alvar Aalto, Kenzo Tange, Hans Hollein, and so on.

In the late 1960s and early 1970s, when the only acceptable architecture style was International Modernism, a number of Iranian architects sporadically searched for a contemporary Iranian architectural language, some coming up with rather promising designs. The French magazine, *L'Architecture d'aujourd'hui*, dedicated an issue in February 1978 to the above-mentioned examples of Iranian contemporary architecture comparing it to the Japanese and Spanish architecture of those days in that it had successfully created an architecture culturally adapted to its own country. The other section of the same issue described the discovery of the significance of Hassan Fathy. In 1976, at the first United Nations Habitat Conference in Vancouver, Canada, the Iranian delegation presented the Habitat Bill of Rights, prepared by Nader Ardalan, Balkrishna Doshi, Lluis Sert, Moshe Safdie and George Candilis, a pioneering document in the architectural discourse of the time. Because of these events, the construction boom due to the oil boom, and the large number of Iranian students attending architecture schools in the West, in the late 1970s, the world became increasingly aware of Iranian architecture and Iranian architects were correspondingly engaging on the international stage.

During the first cycle of the Award, 1978-1980, many Iranian architects were invited to collaborate in various capacities with the Award and participated in the early seminars that led to the establishment of the Award programme. Nader Ardalan, whose book, *The Sense of Unity* (Chicago 1973), written in collaboration with Laleh Bakhtiar, pioneered the understanding of the essence of the architecture of Muslims, served on the first Steering Committee representing a new generation of practicing architects in the Muslim world. Kamran Diba, Nasrine Faghih and Farokh Afshar also participated in the first Award cycle.

Since the first cycle, numerous projects from Iran have been presented as nominations, and in 1980 the restoration of Ali Qapu (pls. 3, 89, 90), Chehel Sutun (pl. 2) and Hasht Behesht (pl. 1) received an Award for its meticulous restoration work and the research work which was published as part of the project and which contributed to our knowledge of the architecture of an important Islamic period. The National Organisation for the Conservation of Historic Monuments of Iran (NOCHMI; now the Iranian Cultural Heritage Organisation – ICHO) carried out the restoration work in collaboration with the Italian Institute for the Middle and Far East (IsMEO), Rome. Eugenio Galdieri was the project architect and the Iranian team was headed by Dr Bagher Ayatolahzadeh Shirazi. Since then, the local restoration experts and craftsmen who trained under the project have used their experience to go on and restore a great number of monuments in Isfahan and other sites in Iran.

In 1986, Shushtar New Town attracted the third Award Master Jury's appreciation. Kamran Diba and his office DAZ had proposed a new approach for designing a company town in Iran (pls. 4, 5). During the 1970s many ambitious industrial projects were launched in Iran and a number of them required new settlements for company employees. Most such programmes envisaged prefabricated apartment blocks in dormitory-style townships next to each factory, attracted by the speed and economy of the construction technique. Diba, through long negotiations, convinced the Iran Housing Company, the governmental client, to build the new settlement for the Karoun Agro-Industry as an extension of the historic city of Shushtar in order to create a real urban life for the employees instead of a new township next to the industrial site. Secondly, he persuaded them to accept a low-rise high-density complex in the spirit of traditional cities instead of the high-rise blocks of Soviet-style company towns. Brick was used as the main construction material, using the architectural vocabulary of the old city of Shushtar instead of the concrete or stone cladding largely used in similar projects. The result was a successful urban design with a central 'multi-faceted pedestrian boulevard' leading to housing clusters and creating lively neighbourhoods.

Unfortunately, only the first phase of the project (1974-1978) was completed as planned before the Revolution and the Iraq-Iran war. However, the project was well received both in Iran and internationally and in the last twenty years the design of a number of new-town projects in Iran has been inspired by this project. Internationally, Shushtar New Town was recognised as an alternative approach to mass housing and the fact that the Award recognised this project has added to its fame. In 1999, Shushtar New Town was chosen for the *At the Turn of the Century* exhibition organised by the Los Angeles Museum of Contemporary Art and featuring the most remarkable architectural projects of the twentieth century.

In the later Award cycles, not many projects from Iran were presented to the jury. This was mainly due to the slower pace of construction in Iran during the first years of the Revolution and the Iran-Iraq war (1980-1988), as well as to the isolation of the country from international fora. While the number of projects presented declined, the Award still closely followed architectural practice in Iran during these years, through its close contacts with a large number of practicing architects as well as architectural schools and government agencies. Kamran Diba and Darab Diba served on Award juries and a number of architects participated in various activities, including Yekta Chahrouzi, Kamran Safamanesh, Homeyra Ettehadieh, Akbar Haji Zargar and Kambiz Navai.

In 2001 the Award Master Jury awarded two projects in Iran: Bagh-e Ferdowsi and New Life for Old Structures. Bagh-e Ferdowsi (pl. 9; designed by Baft-e-Shahr Consultants, Gholamreza Pasban-Hazrat and Farhad Abozzia) was recognised for the creation of a transition space between the high-density urban fabric of Tehran and nature, a space that allows the twelve million inhabitants of this metropolis to benefit from the park's imaginative landscaped design in the foothills of the Alborz mountains.

New Life for Old Structures (pls. 6-8, 12, 16) was awarded for a new approach in using the historic built patrimony for new public usage responding to contemporary urban requirements. The programme, through the collaboration of the ICHO, the body responsible for securing good restoration practice in the country, and the Urban Development and Revitalisation Corporation (UDRC), an agency of the Ministry of Housing and Urban Development, has been responsible for restoring and adaptively reusing non-monumental structures in Yazd and Isfahan, and transferring them to the private or public sector for cultural, educational or tourist usage.

The Award is carefully following the products of the new era of architectural discourse in Iran in recent years and acknowledges the significant role of Iranian architects amongst those shaping the built environment of Muslim societies.

For illustrations of Award-winning projects in Iran mentioned in this article, the reader is referred to pls. 1-9, 12, 16, 89 and 90.

The Art of Revitalisation

SEYYED MOHAMMAD BEHESHTI

Sometimes the eagerness to reach a certain objective causes a person to be deterred from contemplation. Undue haste may prevent him from evaluating the efforts undertaken to move towards the objective, and may even blind him to the purpose of his actions. It is doubtless desirable, even when pursuing a noble aim, to linger on the way and to think about the path that already lies behind, to meditate on what is still ahead, and to remind oneself what the final goal is. Gatherings such as this can grant us a remarkable opportunity to pause and review together what we have done, what we are doing, and what we still have to do.

Human beings have always been curious about their past and have succeeded, to a certain extent, in deciphering many of its secrets. This interest, however, has risen to a new level in modern times, and the preservation of the heritage of the past has taken on a vital importance in today's societies. This has occurred primarily because pre-modern man was involved more in his present time than in his past or future. The past interested him only so far as it directly influenced the present. Today, humanity is greatly concerned about its future, paying less attention to the present and the past. In the quest of a vague future, we have raced through the last centuries and have lost much that lay behind us or along the way. Suddenly, people awoke to an understanding that, in order to have a better future, they have to know their past and preserve its best achievements. This includes the achievements of all cultures and civilisations and implies making use of them for the requirements of modern life-protecting cultural properties of all nations and cultures from destruction by the predominant modernity. With this in mind, men have decided to recreate links with the past, to preserve their heritage, and to pass on this legacy to future generations.

It is undoubtedly laudable to strive towards a better future and to pay attention to the past as an indispensable factor in achieving this future. However, this idea should not conceal a greater truth from us: the past and the future do not exist; what does exist is the present. Imam Ali said: "The past has gone and the future has not come; thus do not miss the transient occasion that lies between these two non-existents". It is correct that the demolition of the past by the relentless forces of modernity is quite disturbing, but it is also important to understand the reasons for its preservation, as well as its employment for the benefit in the present. If we clearly comprehend the benefits of the past and if we understand its advantages for our present, then it will be preserved and delivered to the future as it should be. Humanity and the world are constantly changing. These changes speeded up greatly in modern times. It could not be otherwise because Modernism is nothing other than a constant forward movement. In the course of this progress, at a time when many new achievements already lie buried under a thick layer of even newer accomplishments, when the hurricane of forward movement has uprooted even the mighty trees of recent planting, how can the achievements of earlier epochs survive? Moreover, what use can be made of these achievements in our present and in our future?

Perhaps the following example in the sphere of language can help us to better visualise the situation, as well as to find answers to our questions. Most of us have knowledge of two languages. The first is our mother tongue, and the second the foreign language we have learnt at school or some other educational establishment. However, our relationship with these two languages is never the same. We feel our mother tongue in the depth of our hearts and write poems in it. Even when we listen to poems written by others in our own language, we feel the emotions aroused in us by these poems; our heartstrings tremble at the very sound of the words.

The learning processes of these two languages are also quite different. The native tongue is taught by the mother. Gradually but unceasingly, a word or two at a time, a mother introduces new words to her child and helps her little one in the learning process. Our progress in the mother tongue occurs simultaneously with our progress in recognising the world, and these two processes cannot be separated from each other. Throughout our lives, we increase our vocabularies and our mastery of language, using our personal experience and increasing our knowledge of the world around us. The mother tongue mirrors the perception of the world by the child, who is taking his first steps in it, and the same relations between the world and the child are preserved as this child grows up, as well as throughout his adult life. The mother is a mediator between the child and the world, and it is she who facilitates their introduction to, and acknowledgement of, each other. While teaching the language to her child, a mother never calls upon any knowledge of grammar; moreover, she avoids it. We know that in the past among Arabs there was a recognised practice of sending infants to be taught eloquence and expressiveness by nannies in the desert tribes (called *a'rabi*, meaning "communicative" in Arabic). And indeed these illiterate desert dwellers had a better grasp of the language than the educated town settlers. As to the foreign language, we start to study it when our mentality and attitude towards the world are already formed. Instead of learning this language with the help of our hearts, we use those artificially devised means and methods which make it possible for the student to gain knowledge of a language in a relatively short time — and here a thorough knowledge of grammar is indispensable. Usually we do not write poems in a foreign language except in imitation. By the same token, we do not feel the poems written in a foreign language in our hearts, and do not respond to them with our very essence. We may really like and enjoy these poems, but they will scarcely remind us of our personal experiences, of the times when our spirit gradually learnt the secrets of the universe. The elements of these poems will hardly touch the strings of our hearts, nor make them tremble in the same way as they respond to poems in our native language. Our mother did not teach this language to us. The language she did teach us does conform to the rules of grammar even if they are never explained as such. Hers is the language that is, in fact, the source from which the rules of grammar are derived. Still, she does not teach grammar to her child. What is it, then, that she really teaches?

A mother from Yazd teaches her child the Yazd dialect of the Persian language, but what her child actually learns is to be Iranian and Yazdi. Then this child grows up, goes to school and learns English there. However, he does not learn to be English, because to be English is to see the world through an English mentality, the mentality that took shape under the circumstances surrounding an English child. The Yazdi child may become a great expert in the English language and an outstanding specialist in English literature, but, even so, the masterpieces of Shakespeare, the secrets of which he may have discovered by use of his intellect, would not influence him in the way he is influenced by a simple proverb of the Yazd people or by a line from Hafiz, which he has understood in his heart. We know that what an ordinary Iranian feels towards the poems of Hafiz is quite different from what the most prominent European scholar of Hafiz understands from them. The Persian-speaking Iranian absorbs the spirit of Hafiz's poems and stores it in his heart, while the European scholar of Hafiz considers the mechanical explications of the poems in his mind.

A mother teaches her child the spirit of language, while the teacher gives lessons about the physical aspects of the foreign language. A mother, by teaching the spirit of language to her child, unconsciously conveys to him the spirit and essence of the culture. This spirit and essence learnt by her child – something that forms his character and personality – is what we call "cultural identity". This cultural identity is not taught in educational establishments, nor can it be separated from the person. It is an unconscious part of human nature, locked in to each person throughout his life. These mothers do not have an acquired knowledge of Persian, but possess the innate knowledge of it, because they themselves grew up with it, and their own personality was formed under its influence. Now they give their own children the same innate knowledge of the Persian language and culture. Through this process, the culture and the cultural identity of the entire nation is preserved. This cultural identity, this spirit of nationhood, is not something that has to be developed and changed over time. This spirit can be expressed in various ways and revealed in many different forms.

What is threatened by the sweeping force of Modernism is the body of culture, and not its spirit. However, preserving the body alone will not make possible the protection of the true gem of culture. This gem can be saved only if we consider the body to be a receptacle for the spirit, a particular shape that the culture has taken, and an incarnation of the most important cultural achievements. Only thus can we preserve the true essence and the very spirit of culture, and not only its external form. Only when this body is deemed an incarnation of the immortal spirit and through its preservation the way is paved for the transfer of the spirit of culture can the body itself become eternal. Human history allows the survival only of those things that have been transformed from the superficial into the fundamental, from the acquired into the innate. Only these essential, intrinsic things constitute the greatest legacy of human civilisation and preserve the true spirit and identity of human cultures. If the true knowledge of something is discovered, then it can be preserved, because the innate knowledge is not endangered by external threats. This innate knowledge, or wisdom, lies above the tumultuous tornado of progress and technology. In our era all human efforts and natural factors are aligned with this force of modernity, and there is no power that can resist the devastating storm seeking to sweep away our past. Therefore our only answer rests in an effort to conserve our past by working on the level above this storm – by discovering and preserving the spirit of historical relics.

Historical relics are important because they are both physical evidence of innate knowledge and the vessels that can preserve this knowledge in time. If this is not so, then what is the point in preserving them? If we try to conserve the relic without understanding its real meaning and what it tells us about the cultural spirit of the culture that created it, if we only acquire knowledge about the external characteristics of this artefact and forget about what it contains, our work is meaningless. Of course, we can take care of a relic without understanding the knowledge it conveys, but only if we can be hopeful that future generations will succeed in revealing its true message. It is desirable to attempt to understand the meaning behind each historical relic in the present because, compared to future generations, we are closer to the past. It is easier for us than for our descendants to uncover the message of our ancestors. So let us try to detect it, to preserve it for future generations, and make use of it in the present. Doubtless, acquiring and spreading expertise about the remains of the past is worthy, honourable work, but only if it is part of the greater work of revealing the innate knowledge and the true message of these remains. Otherwise, this work will remind us of an autopsy of a dead body rather than an encounter with a living spirit. Acquisition of empirical factual knowledge at the cost of innate knowledge about the relic arouses in us a false pride for preserving the historical heritage while, in fact, we have preserved only the dead body and failed to find the spirit. It is like building a mausoleum for Ferdowsi, the great Iranian poet, and false-heartedly praising his deeds instead of revealing the underlying message of his work, preserving the spirit of *Shahnamah*, and creating the conditions for reincarnating the spirit of *Shahnamah's* heroes in our contemporaries.

Historical relics are valuable and important because they are the embodiment of the achievements of past cultures and civilisations. These relics and the message they carry deserve the attention and years of efforts of prominent scholars and researchers from all over the world. They deserve to be analysed and discussed during scientific gatherings, like the one in which we are now participating.

Getting back to Ferdowsi's *Shahnamah*, I would like to emphasise again that if we keep the external body of the book or even if we increase our formal knowledge of this book, we can preserve only its form but not its soul. However, if we want to preserve the very spirit of *Shahnamah*, we should search for its intrinsic nature and try to find its innate knowledge. This innate knowledge is the sole source of inspiration for the other epics – the only reason that allows modern authors to create something that can be compared with this masterpiece and that will survive the hurricanes of time, as *Shahnamah* did. One of the ways to preserve a mature tree is to take its picture and forget about the tree itself. However, is it possible to find shelter in the shadow of the picture of the tree, to enjoy the verdure of the tree, the rustle of its leaves, and the creaking of its trunk? To do all of these it is necessary to save the tree itself. Sadly, today we are most often satisfied with the picture of the tree.

Today we preserve historical relics, struggle against their destroyers, and conduct research to increase knowledge about our cultural heritage, but forget about the inner sense of this heritage and the message the relics carry from their creators. Hence we do not increase our innate knowledge about our past. In fact, we avoid seeking this knowledge, and there is little hope that in the future our descendants will make up for our neglect. There are many dead languages and dialects in the world which, for thousands of years, nobody has spoken. There are scholars, of course, who have learnt these languages and can interpret what is written in them. But one of the reasons we call these languages "dead" is because nobody writes poems in them. Poets write poems in living languages. A language is dead when no poem is written in it, even if our knowledge about it is thorough and more extensive than about any living language. We have acquired formal knowledge about dead languages, but lack the innate knowledge about their implicit sense. In fact, this implicit sense is dead and only the explicit form of the dead language has remained. The Persian language is our living, valuable treasure. We write and recite poems in it, love with it, work with it, struggle with it, and live with it. If this language had been only a carrier of information, it would have been dead long ago. If no feeling is expressed in the language, it is nothing more than a complex series of marks – useful, but dead; a language of road signs.

The past has gone, and the future has not arrived. What does exist is the present. If a person is careful about his present, he also paves the way to a good future. Persian literature puts constant emphasis on the value and significance of the present. That does not mean that it neglects the future; it just focuses attention on the most valuable, the most truthful period of time – the present. Indeed, if the present is preserved, then the past becomes meaningful and the future secured. The modern age is a period of carelessness about the present and definitely needs to reconsider its values.

The real progress of humankind is only realised if Man gathers his most prominent achievements throughout his life on this planet, learns the lessons of history, and makes proper use of them to improve all aspects of his life. This is only possible if the experiences gained are transferred from generation to generation. These experiences are transferable if they are transformed into innate knowledge. Moreover, it is possible to maximise the use of previous experiences only by finding the innate knowledge about them. The experiences accumulated by each nation throughout its history synthesise the identity of this nation. A nation can survive and progress only if its identity is preserved and cultivated. Negligence about this identity or attention only to its external manifestations leads it into crisis and, ultimately, to its loss. A nation's historical and cultural identity is like a tree planted by our ancestors. Our duty is not only to keep this tree for ourselves and our descendants, but to help it grow, branch out, and yield sweeter fruits. This is true progress. Only with this approach can we keep our past. Only then does our past not collide with our present, but, rather, is aligned with modern life and becomes indispensable for our development.

The tree of our historical identity is sturdy and strong. It would not wither even if neglected by one generation. This tree is rooted in the spirit of the nation, in the unconscious nature of its people. Its seeds survive even in the souls of those who deny their national and cultural identity; only there these seeds have not germinated. However, it is sufficient that favourable conditions are created: the seeds are then freed and left to sprout. The tree of innate knowledge and historical identity of the nation can survive the hurricanes of time and technical progress; it is not a willow that trembles in the wind. But by neglecting our own identity we cut the branches on which we sit. By this act, we not only deprive ourselves of the valuable experiences accumulated by our ancestors, but also hamper their use by future generations. Attention to the soul of our historical heritage, which is the main component of our historical identity, leads to a better present and, as a result, to a better future for mankind.

As mentioned before, gatherings like this offer us a moment to contemplate our purposes and the ways to achieve them. Evidently our goal in preserving our cultural heritage is to safeguard its soul, its implicit meaning, and the message of its creators. We began our preservation work with this intention, having tried to discover the knowledge of the soul of things, but step by step, while moving along the path, we forget the purpose, limiting ourselves to gaining formal knowledge about the body. We forget to use this knowledge in the service of preserving the jewel of the relic, that is to say, finding the innate knowledge hidden in it. Now it is high time to remind ourselves about our prime goal and to work in a way that helps us to achieve this sacred purpose. As conservation of the body of relics requires the application of scientific and technological methods and tools, the preservation of their souls also needs particular approaches. It needs hearts and wisdom, rather than minds and knowledge. These tools are nothing other than art – the art of preserving the body of cultural remains as a first step towards preserving their souls, the art of finding knowledge about our historical past as a first step to finding the wisdom it contains, the art of 'revitalising' our heritage in the true sense of the word.

For illustrations of Yazd, the reader is referred to pls. 7, 10, 11 and 13-22.

Continuity and Change in the City of Yazd

MOHAMMAD HASSAN KHADEMZADEH

The industrial revolution and modernism not only played an important role in the transformation of eastern and western cities, but also caused changes in the spatial organisation and the formative elements of the city. In this report, Yazd has been studied as a historical-cultural desert city and as a city with highly complicated traditional elements as well as large areas of new development.

THE GEOGRAPHICAL SITUATION OF THE CITY OF YAZD

Yazd is located in the centre of Iran, to the east of Isfahan and south of Kavir Loot, at an altitude of twelve hundred metres above sea level. The population of the city numbers about four hundred thousand and the climate is desert and semi-desert with hot, dry summers and hot, cold winters. Up until the seventh century it had, though, enjoyed a pleasant climate, with green countryside and forests linking it to Kerman; however, due to atmospheric changes and the irregular use of land, it slowly changed into a dry and infertile desert area. Lack of rain in the region means there is no suitable vegetation and farmers have no alternative but to use deep wells and subterranean canals to provide water for their lands. Yazd is mentioned in important books such as *Masalek and Mamalek, Souratolarz* and the *Travels of Marco Polo* (1272).

STRUCTURAL CHANGES IN THE CITY OF YAZD

The enclosed part of the city of Yazd was developed in different stages until the end of the fourteenth century. According to the records, before Islam and during the Achaemenid period (550 to 330 BC) the city was known as Issatis and was located where Yazd stands today, although no valid and reliable documents have survived. According to another historical record, the development of Yazd goes back to the time of Alexander, who founded a prison here and the city was called Kasah (both recorded in Afshar, 1966). According to another historical report in the *History of Yazd* by Iraj Afshar (1995), the city was developed by a Sassanid prince named Yazdgerd and might have been named after him. In the seventh century AD, during the time of the third caliph of Islam (Othman), the city fell to Muslim troops. At that time, Yazd was equal in importance to Aghda, Meybod, Hafadar and Fahraj. It can be said that the development and first expansion of Yazd into a prestigious and integrated city dates back to the eleventh century AD with the construction of massive castles and gates around the city, creating a new identity. Like many other cities in Iran, the structure and morphology of the city did not change greatly during the Mongol period (AD 1256-1346). A number of new buildings were built in the fourteenth century, while during the Muzzaffarid dynasty the city started growing towards the south and south-west and a new wall with seven gates was also built. Historical documents have named three reasons for the city's tendency to develop in these directions: Masserat (1997) believes that first, the sand wind blows from the north; second, suitable land for building was readily available in the south and south-west; and third, water underground flows from the south and south-west towards the city. The Amir Chakhmagh Complex (pls. 10, 19), including the mosque, bazaar and water basin, was built around a large square in the south-east of the city at the beginning of the fifteenth century, and, gradually, the centre of the city was transferred away from the great mosque (Masjid Jami'; pls. 11, 15, 18, 20, 21) and its immediate neighbourhood.

The stages in the transfer of the city centre are quite different to development in other Islamic cities in Iran, such as Isfahan, which was developed around an old great mosque (Masjid Jami'). The bazaar, which had first developed near Masjid Jami', was established near the southern gates, abutting the back of the city walls and fortifications to reach Amir Chakhmagh. The bazaar grew rapidly and an active trading centre was formed in this district.

Compared to other Iranian cities, such as Isfahan, Shiraz, Kerman, or Tabriz, Yazd did not develop much during the Safavid dynasty (AD 1501-1773) and few buildings were built. Another complex, named the Shah Tahmasb that included other service spaces, was built in 1790, but unlike Amir Chakhmagh Square, it was built to the south-west of the city wall. These two squares were connected via a dense trading district. The city centre remained in the same place and the city started growing around the city walls, developing to the west and south-west with the addition of new neighbourhoods.

During the Zand and Qajar periods, the city continued to develop southwards as exemplified by the complex consisting of a square, school, public bath and Bazaar-e Khan. In 1815, a great wall was built that enclosed the whole city, but it never acted as a strong containing border and the city continued its development towards the south and south-west.

Despite new street construction in the old part of the city during the Pahlavi dynasty, the importance and core value of Yazd remained intact. Gradually, though, by the end of the Pahlavi period, city development again accelerated; few changes were made in the structure of the historical city and its role in the social and economic life of the city decreased and was transferred to more developed parts of it. The Islamic Revolution (1979) and the conditions that governed it intensified this through:
- the growth of the urban population and the migration of villagers;
- land transfer around the city and its irregular expansion;

- changes in economic and social conditions so that the traditional city was preserved only within the scope of its valuable historical elements. Although attention to the old structure of the city was increasing in the theoretical discourse and among specialised groups, new construction continued.

A DETAILED PLAN FOR THE PRESERVATION OF OLD YAZD

A Detailed Plan for the old city was drawn up in two stages with the first covering the central area (the Fahadan block and peripheral blocks) and the second, the remaining sections. The proposal attempted to coordinate and match change to the cultural-historical value of given zones.

NAGHIB OL-ASHRAF ALLEY

The plan calls for improved car (and truck) access in order to facilitate the use of modern construction techniques in the area and also to directly improve the welfare of local residents. For several reasons, less than ten percent of the changes planned in the communication network were executed.

THE RESTORATION OF IMPORTANT BUILDINGS

The restoration of significant buildings was another stage in the process involving both change and continuity in the traditional urban fabric. Although, at the outset, the Iranian Cultural Heritage Organisation (ICHO) and the Faculty of Architecture and Urban Development played an effective role in the development of this objective, this undertaking has currently expanded to include both governmental and private participation. A number of historical residential areas have been transformed into administrative spaces. By restoring the Lari-ha House (Khaneh Lari-ha; pl. 14) and then expanding work to the buildings located around it, the ICHO has restored a vast area. Establishing the Faculty of Architecture here has meant both an educational utilisation of the cultural environment and a huge increase of interest through the students' movement.

Other examples of adaptive reuse include the transformation of a house into an educational establishment for teaching the Koran to children; changing a historic public bath into a restaurant and tea house; transforming the ruins of a historical caravanserai and front yard of the Ziaieh School into a public park; and changing a number of evacuated residential units into public passages by maintaining the structure and improving the Abolmaali block.

PROJECT STAGE

The irregular growth and development of the city was one of the main factors that caused a lack of efficiency in urban management. Gradually, greater focus was placed on inner development, aiming at achieving the goal of economic and social improvement in the traditional city. In this stage, through identifying suitable areas, some parts of the traditional city were repossessed by governmental authorities (Housing and Urban Development Department and Maskansazan Company), providing residences for housing applicants. Despite identifying and defining many potential projects, only one has been fully executed and another is under construction. Obviously, evaluating these experiences will be of high importance in re-evaluating the theoretical basis for this work.

TRADITIONAL CITY MANAGEMENT STAGE

The goals of this phase are:
- to set long- and short-term plans, strategies and policies and move towards provincial/national agreements;
- to determine and define the status of the development of the city and province;
- to coordinate executive systems and determine the responsibility of each one in achieving the predicted goals;
- to encourage resident participation in discussions, decision making and execution;
- to improve financial resources through national and local credits as well as popular participation and attracting investments in different economic sectors that would be compatible with traditional city management. A council for restoring historic buildings in the province and a guidance council have been created.

Although all the expectations arising from this discourse have not yet been fulfilled, it is fervently hoped that it can stimulate the necessary changes for continuing to improve life in the traditional city.

For illustrations of Yazd, the reader is referred to pls. 7, 10, 11 and 13-22.

Trends in Modern Iranian Architecture

DARAB DIBA AND MOZAYAN DEHBASHI

A new age in Iranian architecture began with the rise of the Safavid dynasty. Economically robust and politically stable, this period saw a flourishing growth of theological sciences. Traditional architecture evolved in its patterns and methods leaving its impact on the architecture of the following periods.

The appearance of new patterns based on geometrical networks in the development of cities gave order to open urban spaces, and took into account the conservation of natural elements (water and plants) within cities. The establishment of distinctive public spaces is one of the most important urban features of the Safavid period, as manifested for example in Naghsh-e Jahan Square, Chahar Bagh and the royal gardens of Isfahan.

Distinctive monuments like the Sheikh Lotfallah (1603), Hasht Behesht (Eight Paradise Palace) (1699; pl. 1) and the Chahar Bagh School (1714) appeared in Isfahan and other cities. This extensive development of architecture was rooted in Persian culture and took form in the design of schools, baths, houses, caravanserai and other urban spaces such as bazaars and squares. It continued until the end of the Qajar reign.

The confrontation of Iran with western civilisation that began with the Qajar reign brought political and social modernisation to Iran during the period stretching from 1800 to 1979. This upheaval naturally engendered a transformation of architecture, and, eventually, the rise of a novel architecture in Iran. The spaces that Iranians are presently living in today were born of this process that we propose to review in relation to trends in the contemporary architecture of Iran.

THE QAJAR ERA (1800-1925)

The first stage of Iran's modern architectural development took place during the Qajar period. It happened as a result of the reforms enacted by the princesses and authorities such as Abbas Mirza, Mirza Taghi Khan Amir Kabir and intellectuals like Mirza Malcolm Khan, Mirza Fathali Khan Akhondzadeh and those who pursued the rational rule of law and the development of public education and welfare. With economic independence as their real aim these authorities laid the groundwork for the appearance of a new Persian architecture. The increase in communications between

Iran and Europe allowed increasing acquaintance with European art and architecture, which became apparent in the design of government monuments like the Shams al-Emareh (1861) and the Golestan Palace (1870).

THE PAHLAVI ERA (1925-1979)

With the rule of the Pahlavi dynasty, architecture was modernised in a new way. Socio-political planning under the authoritative rule of government with the aid of westerners was the style of the period. During the rule of Reza Shah (1925-1941) the industrialisation of the country began to take place; road and rail networks were built, in conjunction with a marked Europeanisation of social behaviour. Education, the economy, and culture all figured on the agenda of Reza Shah under the influence of the West, while the reconstruction efforts in Turkey headed by Mustafa Atatürk led to imitation and rivalry. During the two decades of Reza Shah's rule, the government played an active role in the execution of civil projects. Western architects were invited to design new buildings for the first time, and the reconstruction plans were executed with great speed. As a result the traditional design of many cities changed significantly.

This period also saw the development of factories, government offices and universities, and the use of new building materials like steel, cement and glass. New construction techniques brought with them a variety of styles or trends of European and Iranian origin.

'ECLECTIC FUSION' WITH AN EMPHASIS ON IRANIAN ARCHITECTURE

This trend embodied nationalistic and progressive goals and looked back to the example of pre-Islamic architecture. It was also strongly influenced by nineteenth-century Neoclassical European architecture. This style was applied to the design of governmental buildings or schools and banks and its influence was particularly felt in the plans of the buildings through an application of symmetry, hierarchy and geometric forms: buildings like the National Police Headquarters (1933) are a good example. The combination of these two approaches — European and Iranian — was such that European architecture, and especially the Neoclassical style, found a specific expression of its own. The entry gateways of Maidan Mashgh (1931) and Hassan Abad Square (1935) are superior examples of this trend.

PURELY EUROPEAN ARCHITECTURE

This tendency developed as a result of the progressive aims of certain intellectuals. In this type of architecture there was no sign or influence of Persian forms. It was often brought to Iran without any adjustments. Tehran Railway Station (1937), the Ministry of Justice (1938), the University Departments of Medicine and Law, and Tehran University's Campus (1934) are examples of this trend under the reign of the first Pahlavi. Mohsen Foroughi, Vartan Hovanesian, Ali Sadegh, Kayghobad Zafar Bakhtiar, Paul Abkar, Gabriel Gevorkian, and Iraj Moshiri were the proponents of this process.

MOHAMMAD REZA SHAH (1941-1979)

Mohammad Reza Pahlavi rose to power in 1941, but from that year to 1953 a limited amount of development occurred due to political conditions in the country. After 1953, and especially from 1969 to 1979 with the aid of substantial oil income, important strides were made in economics, education, health and medicine. Because of the economic consequences of the government's policies, development became equivalent to investment. The cultural dimension of this work was less well considered, and one of its consequences was the hurried and uncalculated importation of western ways.

The establishment of modern educational institutions like the School of Fine Arts encouraged a vogue for modern western architecture. Meanwhile socio-political reasoning pushed Iran towards industrialisation, and led to the speedy growth of urban areas. In this respect two trends can be analysed here.

THE DEVELOPMENT OF THE SCHOOL OF MODERNISM AND THE INTERNATIONAL STYLE IN ARCHITECTURE (1941-1979)

This process, which occurred in the design of some structures from 1953 to 1963, was now applied to almost all buildings. During this period numerous governmental and commercial buildings were erected and many residences were built without consideration for local characteristics or climatic conditions, in Tehran and in other cities like Tabriz, Yazd, Mashhad and Kashan.

It is worth noting that during these decades a profit-making attitude aimed at faster, cheaper construction led to the exclusion of all ornamental elements and the use of a minimum variety of materials (brick, steel and glass), and paved the way for developers to build and sell increasingly uniform structures regardless of location. Unfortunately, the problems that this method entailed continue to have an impact in contemporary Iran.

Nevertheless, well beyond the range of the developers, monuments like the Senate (Islamic parliament, Mohsen Foroughi and Heydar Ghiaï, 1959) and the Ministry of Oil building (Yahya Ettehadieh and Abdolaziz Farmanfarmaian, 1969) were built under the influence of advanced international Modernism, and are cited today as distinct examples of modern Iranian architecture.

This distinct presence of international Modernism continued until 1979, and we can see its influence in buildings such as the Takhti (Amjadieh Stadium, 1966), the City Theatre (1971), the Azadi Sports Compound (1974), and the Ministry of Agriculture (1975), all designed by reputable architects such as Jahanguir Darvish, Ali Sardar Afkhami and Abdolaziz Farmanfarmaian.

THE DIALOGUE BETWEEN TRADITION AND MODERNISM (1965-1979)

Although the International Style and the school of Modernism were strongly promoted by architectural schools and firms like Abdolalziz Farmanfarmaian, efforts to achieve a cultural identity in Iranian architecture advanced through the work of architects like Houshang Seyhoun, Kamran Diba, Hossein Amanat and Nader Ardalan.

By designing tombs for famous scientific and literary figures, like Avicenna's tomb in the city of Hamedan, or Khayam's tomb in the city of Neyshabur, Houshang Seyhoun was one of the first architects during the period 1950 to 1965 who took a step beyond international architecture and created a common language linking modern architecture and traditional Iranian designs. Paying attention to pure geometrical volumes he achieved a metaphoric expression.

In the middle of the 1960s new discourses were gradually introduced in professional and educational gatherings through the presence of individuals like Nader Ardalan and Kamran Diba in which history and tradition were considered as indispensable parts of the Iranian architectural identity. Nader Ardalan and Laleh Bakhtiar's research for the book *The Sense of Unity* was also influential and, as a result, some exemplary buildings related to this trend came into existence, such as the Iran Centre for Management Studies (today the Imam Sadegh University) designed by Nader Ardalan (pl. 26); the University of Jondi Shapour (Ahvaz, 1968); the new city of Shushtar (1974; pls. 4, 5) and the Tehran Museum of Contemporary Art designed by Kamran Diba (pl. 25). The Iran Centre of Management in particular was designed with the inspiration of universal principles and reference to a specifically Iranian relation of space with nature. The Tehran Museum of Contemporary Art employs introversion in its principles of organisation and the design of spatial elements, with tall light wells to remind visitors of desert wind catchers, a clear reference to Iranian architecture. The design of the Shushtar residential compounds was inspired by the principles of organisation and typology of traditional Iranian cities and the use of local material adjusted to the climate.

In short, what appeared at the end of the Pahlavi era in cities was an inharmonious combination of the developers' build-and-sell architecture and western modern designs. Nevertheless, efforts had been made to affirm Iranian cultural identity during the early Pahlavi era. During the second Pahlavi reign individual tendencies, manifested in the works of Ardalan or Diba, did not develop into stable trends permitting the emergence of a genuinely Iranian modern architecture.

THE ISLAMIC REPUBLIC (1974-TO DATE)

The political and social events of 1979 created a rupture between architecture before and after the Revolution. New viewpoints related to cultural, national or religious ideals emerged. The eight-year-long Iran-Iraq war created many social and economic disturbances that influenced architecture and urban planning. Amongst these were changes in the educational system, the halt in many of the investments in civil affairs, and the closing of many architectural firms. The emigration of a number of university professors and architects also had an impact during the years after the Revolution. The effort to create an Islamic identity became a dominant concern.

A certain pluralism and a variety of points of views are a special feature of architecture during the two decades after the Revolution, and especially during the 1990s. On the one hand, creating architecture and urban planning to correspond with the values and ideals of Islamic society was an essential element in this period. On the other hand, western-influenced trends like Post-Modernism and Deconstructivism, also played a role in Iranian architecture. Several trends can be distinguished.

REVITALISATION / REJUVENATION

During the 1980s and 1990s efforts to rejuvenate Islamic culture were a priority. The use of materials like brickwork and tiles, and ornamental elements like moulding and calligraphy, were part of the effort to give Islamic spirit to buildings. This approach was not confined to specifically Islamic architectural types, and forms like central gardens, domes, or arches were frequently seen.

Many of the residential and governmental buildings in Tehran and other cities were built under this influence. The shrine of Imam Khomeini (1991), the Organisation of the Hajj (1988) and the Sharif University Mosque (2000) in Tehran are distinct examples of this style. It is reasonable to say that this trend, essentially a superficial imitation of past patterns and forms detached from time and place, cannot have a lasting place in contemporary Iranian architecture.

ECLECTICISM RELATED TO WESTERN POST-MODERN ARCHITECTURE

In the mid-1980s under the influence of western architecture an eclectic architecture came into existence with a number of architects taking elements of Iranian architecture and combining them eclectically with the western Post-Modern style. Certain buildings displayed influences ranging from Post-Modern architecture to Neoclassicism and Iranian architecture, especially from the Qajar era. Architectural elements from both cultures were applied to façades and plans were designed to orderly geometrical forms and systems. The Bureau for Members of Parliament (1990), the Allame Dehkhoda University in Qazvin (1993; pl. 27), the Honarestan in Karaj (1991-1993), the Social Hall of the Pasture Institute (1989) and the dormitories of the University of Yazd are particular examples of this trend.

In some buildings a fusion of modern and contemporary architecture was attempted. The result was the creation of buildings like the Cultural Centre of Kerman and the Jolfa residential complex in Isfahan. Sometimes these structures included the repetition of traditional Iranian elements like arches, wind catchers, domes and half-domes and the use of variations of brickwork next to space frames. As such it was an attempt to create a variegated and Iranian spirit, but at the cost of a surprisingly eclectic fusion. A number of buildings managed only to reflect western Post-Modernism in Iran: in this category, the Armita Tower for offices can be mentioned (pl. 29).

This architecture became very popular in the developers' build-and-sell scheme, due to a lack of evolution in building technology and a lack of rules and regulations. Its eclectic language became an instrument for the false, profit-worshipping attitude of the property and housing construction market in cities. The result was the flourishing of a glittering, worthless architecture, which made clumsy copies of most of the world architectural styles. Many residential buildings, especially of the high-rise variety, fall into this category.

In the Post-Modern style some works nonetheless have special importance. The Sports Complex of the city of Rafsanjan (2001; pl. 35) designed by S. Hadi Mirmiran is an example of a design that has been developed on the basis of old Iranian architecture while attempting to create architecture with a Persian identity.

THE PERMANENCE OF MODERN ARCHITECTURE
The western school of modern architecture has been the most influential force from the outset of the Pahlavi era until today. It is still a significant factor in contemporary Iranian architecture. Modern architecture since the Revolution has been formed in response to economic trends, and construction rules and regulations. These buildings follow the fundamental principles of western modern architecture such as pragmatic functionalism, in favour of simplicity (exclusion of ornaments), a generous use of glass for cladding, and a use of construction materials that makes them different from their predecessors.

With respect to this trend the following buildings can be mentioned: the Telecommunications building located on Yousef Abad Avenue in Tehran (1994; pl. 28) which has an appropriate functionalism; the Iranian National Library (1996) and many commercial structures in Tehran such as the office building by Mr Maghzi.

THE APPEARANCE OF SPECIAL TRENDS
Defining the correct position of Iranian Islamic architecture in the post-modern world elicits various points of view. The increasing importance of literature related to linguistic philosophy, post-constructivism, cultural relativism, and the 'end of ideology' has instigated a sort of mental inflammation in the community of Iranian architects. A pragmatism abstracted from the environment is one of the trends that has developed in this respect and its most important specifications are as follows.

SCIENTIFIC-FUNCTIONAL (ABSTRACTED FROM THE ENVIRONMENT)
This view, inspired by literary, philosophical and mathematical theories for explaining the 'concept' in the creation of works originated from the Deconstructivist movement and the developments

inspired by computers in western architectural literature. Architectural space has been reduced to scientific mathematical space. Environmental comparisons, including history and local tradition are not considered by these theories. At the utmost, despite discussions and literature that explain the 'Iranian-ness' of the projects, they are mere repetitions of the work of well-known western architects such as Zaha Hadid, Peter Eisenman, Daniel Libeskind, and others. Due to the limitations of construction technology and implementation in Iran, these works have remained three dimensional computer images.

In some schools of architecture this visually very attractive trend has been disseminated, albeit without any deep comprehension of this type of western architecture. Those who defend this kind of thought resort to special rationalisations by linking the theoretical aspects of the trend to some philosophical, religious Iranian grounds. They thus try to give legitimacy and credibility to contemporary Iranian architecture.

CREATING A DIALOGUE BETWEEN IRANIAN ARCHITECTURE AND WORLD ARCHITECTURE

If, during the Pahlavi era, Iranians regarded the achievements of western civilisation as a model and pursued total imitation of western designs, this was merely a special feature of progressive Iranian architecture. During the years that have followed the Revolution, in the struggle to achieve cultural identity, Iranian architects have turned towards revitalisation/rejuvenation and fusion or eclecticism. Presently, the trend that is emerging among architects is one accompanied by wide analysis and precise criticism. They are taking strides towards recognising 'real' cultures, and see solutions in the opening of minds towards the world at large.

In the sense that they view the achievements of western civilisation not as a model but as part of human heritage and seek to be contemporary with the people of their own times this is an interesting path. By benefiting from their thinking, by incorporating the technological facilities of today, together with inspirations from universal Iranian architecture as an abstract expression, architects may indeed be able to create a truly Iranian contemporary architecture.

It seems that with this new process of Iranian contemporary architecture, which is searching for the gist of universal art, it might be possible to create more distinctive works than in the past. Maybe enumerating a few examples, such as the Sports Complex of the city of Rafsanjan (pl. 35), the Jamshidieh Park, the Embassy of the Islamic Republic of Iran in Berlin (pl. 33), the Hafezieh residences in the Sadabad palace complex (pl. 34), the Embassy of the Islamic Republic of Iran in Australia and the Jolfa residential compound of Isfahan might reveal evidence of the beginnings of this trend. It is a process that is expected to become one of the main trends in contemporary Iranian architecture.

For illustrations of this article, the reader is referred to pls. 1, 4, 5, 23-29 and 33-35.

Public Buildings in Iran: 1920 to the Present

S. HADI MIRMIRAN

This paper deals with contemporary Iranian architecture, with a focus on public buildings, and briefly looks at different periods of Iran's new architecture and the significant works that have emerged during these periods.

The new movement in Iranian architecture began about eighty years ago, during the 1920s. At that time, following the political transformations in the country and along with changes in social and economic conditions, the image of its cities changed. In response to the requirements of modern living, new building types such as banks, universities and factory buildings emerged. This time span of eighty years can be divided into four distinct periods:

- from about 1920 to 1940;
- from about 1940 to 1970;
- from about 1970 to 1979;
- from 1979 to date.

During the first period, from 1920 to 1940, the most important buildings were built under the patronage of the government and by foreign architects. These buildings were massive, voluminous and monumental and were intended to renew the old Iranian architecture, but this intention was limited to a superficial repetition of architectural forms, elements and motives particularly those of Achaemenid and Sassanid periods. Except for a few buildings such as the Iran Bastan Museum by André Godard with Maxim Siroux (pl. 24), the University of Tehran Campus by André Godard and the Palace of Justice by Gabriel Gevorkian, the buildings of this period lack any significant architectural value.

The next period began in 1940 and continued until 1970. The prominent buildings of this period were created in compliance with the principles of modern architecture by Iranian architects who were trained abroad such as Mohsen Foroughi, Houshang Seyhoun and Abdolaziz Farmanfarmaian. Although their buildings follow the principles of modern architecture their reference to old Iranian architecture presents a much higher quality using the patterns and architectural geometry of Iran. However, this period was unable to create any world-class modern architecture, nor was it completely successful in the use of Iranian architectural principles and ideas.

The third period began in 1970 and coincided with an era when the Modern Movement faced serious confrontations, and a historicist approach towards architecture was taking shape within the Modern Movement. In the meanwhile, several Iranian architects attempted to engender stronger ties with tradition in their works. Compared to the works of past periods, these are more accomplished insofar as their relationship with tradition is concerned.

After the emergence of the Post-Modern movement in world architecture, which was almost synchronous with the Islamic Revolution in Iran, two equally important factors gave birth to a new era of Iranian architecture. On the one hand, Iranian architects attempted to create an independent identity derived from Iran's architectural heritage while, on the other, Post-Modern architecture had a serious interest in traditional architecture of different nations. The union of these two factors resulted in an architecture of a Post-Modern style that indulged in traditional, particularly Islamic, motifs and elements. But then again this approach towards traditional architecture remained on the surface and Post-Modern clichés had an overwhelming presence in these works.

During the last decade, following the failure of various architects of these periods both in creating works on a global scale and in creative deployment of traditional principles, a group of Iranian architects initiated a new search based on past efforts that has shaped a progressive new movement in Iranian architecture today. Unfortunately, due to a lack of proper communication and intellectual interaction between the architects of the newly born movement, despite many common themes in their approaches and methods, this trend is not yet well defined and has no clear architectural agenda. Therefore, I have chosen some examples of this movement to comment on.

These works can be subdivided into three groups. The first group consists of works that offer a new interpretation of traditional patterns. Outstanding examples are the three proposals for the Islamic Republic of Iran Academies' Complex by S. Hadi Mirmiran, Ali Akbar Saremi and Darab Diba, and a proposal for the History Museum of Khurasan by M. A. Mirfendereski.

The second group includes works where the use of architectural heritage is not restricted to principles and prototypes of traditional architecture, but addresses Iranian culture on a broader scale with its myths, concepts, cultural contents and memories. These works have benefited from other artistic fields such as poetry and literature for intellectual innovation in architecture. Outstanding examples of this group are the proposals for the Iranian National Library competition by S. Hadi Mirmiran, Kamran Safamanesh (pl. 31) and Farhad Ahmadi; the Imam Khomeini International Airport Terminal by Bahram Shirdel, and the National Museum of Water by S. Hadi Mirmiran.

The third group consists of projects designed during the last five years (1997-2002). These projects have attempted to comply with new global paradigms and to confront the world's progressive architectural discourse, while at the same time deeply benefiting from traditional architecture. Some significant examples of this group are the Tehran BAR Association building in Tehran by S. Hadi Mirmiran (pl. 30); the Department of Persian Language in Daka by Kamran Safamanesh; the Embassy of the Islamic Republic of Iran in Albania by Ali Akbar Saremi; the Embassy of the Islamic Republic of Iran in Sweden by Farhad Ahmadi; the Embassy of the Islamic Republic of Iran in Brazil by Bahram Shirdel; the Presidential Bureau of Technological Collaborations by Bahram Shirdel, and the General Consulate of the Islamic Republic of Iran in Frankfurt by S. Hadi Mirmiran.

In this brief review of the architecture of this eighty-year period, four main issues stand out:
- during the past eighty years, Iranian architecture has lagged behind in the footsteps of modern and Post-Modern architecture without enough knowledge about these movements;
- all architects of this period have been more or less concerned that their architecture should have a serious orientation towards the historical and architectural heritage of Iran;
- the ideal of presenting projects at a global level and contributing to the progress of world architecture has been intensified during the past three decades;
- a large number of contemporary Iranian architects believe that merely relying on the great architectural heritage of this country and developing its principles will be enough to engender an architectural movement, which could have a global role. The superficial use of past forms and typologies has now been changed to a more abstract and deeper presence in their works and today Iranian architects try not only to place themselves with the world's innovative architectural movements but also to preserve the essence of Iranian culture in their works.

For illustrations of this article, the reader is referred to pls. 24 and 30-35.

2.

1-3. Italian Institute for the Middle
and Far East (IsMEO; Eugenio Galdieri)
and the National Organisation
for the Conservation of Historic Monuments
of Iran (NOCHMI; Bagher Shirazi),
restoration of Hasht Behesht, Chehel Sutun
and Ali Qapu, Isfahan, Iran, 1977.

Previous page
1. Hasht Behesht (1699), Isfahan, Iran,
restored in 1977.

2. Chehel Sutun (1667), Isfahan, Iran,
restored in 1977.

3. Ali Qapu (1660), Isfahan, Iran,
restored in 1977.

3.

4, 5. Daz/Kamran Diba,
Shushtar New Town,
Shushtar, Iran, 1974-1978.

4.

5.

6.

7.

6-8. Iranian Cultural Heritage
Organisation (ICHO)
and the Urban Development
and Revitalisation Corporation
(UDRC), New Life for Old
Structures programme, various
locations, Iran, 1992-ongoing.

6. Nilforooshan House
(19th century), Isfahan, Iran,
restored in 1998.

7. Moayed Alaai House
(19th century), Yazd, Iran,
restored in 1997.

8. Modjtahedzadeh House
(19th century), Isfahan, Iran,
restored in 1992.

8.

9.

9. Baft-e-Shahr Consultants, Bagh-e Ferdowsi,
Tehran, Iran, 2000.

10.

11.

10. Amir Chakhmagh Complex (15th century), Yazd, Iran.

11. Masjid Jami' (14th century) in the background, Yazd, Iran.

12. Iranian Cultural Heritage Organisation (ICHO) and the Urban Development and Revitalisation Corporation (UDRC), New Life for Old Structures programme, Modjtahedzadeh House (19th century), Isfahan, Iran, restored in 1992.

13. Badgirs (wind catchers), Yazd, Iran.

12.

13.

14.

15.

16.

14. Iranian Cultural Heritage Organisation (ICHO), restoration of Lari-ha House (19th century), Yazd, Iran.

15. Masjid Jami' (14th century), Yazd, Iran.

16. Iranian Cultural Heritage Organisation (ICHO) and the Urban Development and Revitalisation Corporation (UDRC), New Life for Old Structures programme, Hammam Khan (19th century), Yazd, Iran, restored in 1997.

17. A general view of Yazd, Iran.

18. The courtyard of Masjid Jami' (14th century), Yazd, Iran.

17.

18.

20.

21.

22.

19. Amir Chakhmagh Complex (15th century), Yazd, Iran.

20, 21. Masjid Jami' (14th century), Yazd, Iran.

22. Mahmoodi House (19th century), Yazd, Iran.

23.

23. Hossein Amanat, Azadi Monument, Tehran, Iran, 1974.

24.

25.

24. André Godard with Maxim Siroux, Iran Bastan Museum,
Tehran, Iran, 1931-1936.

25. Kamran Diba, Tehran Museum of Contemporary Art,
Tehran, Iran, 1976.

26.

26. Mandala Consultants/Nader Ardalan,
Iran Centre for Management Studies, Tehran, Iran, 1974.

27. Bavand Consultants, Allame Dehkhoda
University, Qazvin, Iran, 1989.

28. Atec Consultants, Telecommunications Building,
Tehran, Iran, 1994.

29. Sharestan Consultants, Armita Tower,
Tehran, Iran, 1997.

27.

28.

29.

30.

31.

32.

33.

35.

34.

30. S. Hadi Mirmiran, Tehran BAR Association, Tehran, Iran, 2000.

31. Kamran Safamanesh, Iranian National Library competition, Tehran, design 1995.

32. S. Hadi Mirmiran, Export Development Bank of Iran, Tehran, design 1997.

33. Darab Diba/Safaverdi Associates, Embassy of the Islamic Republic of Iran, Berlin, Germany, 2004.

34. Bavand Consultants/Hossein Zeineddin, Hafezieh Complex, Tehran, Iran, 1998.

35. S. Hadi Mirmiran, Sports Complex, Rafsanjan, Iran, 2001.

RESTORING THE CITY: BUILDING ANEW

Revitalise to Survive: the Old City of Jerusalem

SHADIA TOUQAN

THE OLD CITY NOW

On the surface, problems in the Old City of Jerusalem seem characteristic and prototypical of problems shared in many historic cities in Arab and Islamic countries.

The dynamics of modern-day needs, rapid population growth, increased pressure on overloaded services, lack of technical and financial resources to enable appropriate rehabilitation and maintenance of the building stock, the replacement of the original community of the historic city by the influx of lower income groups, overcrowding, high unemployment and low expectations are all simply indicators of the serious sickness a historic city suffers from. Such indicators are usually representative of many historic cities; however, after the diagnosis of these symptoms in Jerusalem it becomes clear that an additional factor contributed to and accelerated the deterioration process. The political and security conditions prevailing in Palestine, particularly in Jerusalem and more specifically in and around the Old City, have created an atmosphere of fear and despair resulting in a fierce fight for space, symbols of identity and in many cases mere survival.

In the past few years, and following the Israeli measures against Palestinian citizens of Jerusalem, the city witnessed an influx of Jerusalem identity card (ID) holders returning to live in the city. The original and rightful residents of Jerusalem, who lived and worked in the outskirts or nearby areas of Jerusalem, continued to be under threat of losing their IDs and subsequently their rights in the city. This sudden population increase resulted in housing shortage for the lower income groups who could not afford the high rents and taxes of more affluent areas in East Jerusalem. The difficulties and obstacles the Palestinians face in obtaining building permits within the municipal boundaries as defined by the occupation authorities aggravate the shortage.

Consequently, thousands of Jerusalem ID holders are seeking shelter in the Old City where they can stay with relatives, rent cheaply or even live as squatters in empty or abandoned historic buildings and monuments within the city walls. There are no accurate statistics to show the number of people who have moved back to live in Jerusalem, but it is evident that the Israeli policy backfired and resulted in an increase rather than a decrease in the number of the Palestinian population in Jerusalem.

The increase in the population in the Old City is accompanied by increased pressure for accommodation and basic services. This has resulted in unplanned vertical and horizontal expansions and additions to existing buildings implemented by the residents without technical guidance or supervision. Such a trend is affecting the physical shape and condition of the buildings and in many cases inflicting irreparable damage on the historic and cultural 'value' of their new homes.

The urban fabric of the Old City of Jerusalem is still generally intact in spite of years of neglect, natural and man-made disasters and unplanned and sometimes unwelcome change of use. Many old *madrasas* (schools) have been converted to residences, mausoleums to houses, palaces to schools and warehouses. The structure of these buildings is mainly solid and although stone walls and façades have deteriorated due to dampness, humidity and pollution, most buildings can be salvaged with the proper care and appropriate restoration techniques. The worst cases were found in buildings that had been abandoned or remained unused for a long time.

It is evident that continued use of a building (whether suitable or unsuitable, planned or arbitrary) allows for some form of maintenance, for ventilation and heating, which helps to protect it. The situation is far from ideal, but also far from disastrous.

The building stock that belongs to certain institutions (Muslim or Christian Waqf) has fared better in terms of the quality of restoration work as it was generally carried out by professionals. However, the fact that most of the repair/restoration work in the city is executed by users without technical guidance and supervision, poses the question to us agencies involved in the revitalisation process about what can be done to improve the quality of work carried out by the informal sector.

While one cannot control what others do, in the absence of Palestinian legislative and executive authority in Jerusalem, it is important to find the means to address the issue of 'informal restoration'. This could be helped through public awareness campaigns, community participation in the decision-making process and special training programmes: all should depend on the active participation of the media.

THE ROLE OF THE OLD CITY OF JERUSALEM REVITALISATION PROGRAMME (OCJRP)
In 1995, the Technical Office of the Welfare Association was established to implement a comprehensive programme for the Revitalisation of the Old City of Jerusalem. The programme is co-funded by the Arab Fund for Social and Economic Development, the Welfare Association and other Arab and international sources.

The original programme had five main components: emergency restoration of houses and monuments under physical and/or political threat; total restoration, which includes housing renewal and adaptive reuse; a revitalisation plan for the Old City based on extensive surveys and comprehensive sectoral studies which created a data base for the Old City; a training programme for professionals and craftsmen; and a community outreach programme.

The Technical Office approach involves all issues related to preservation and revitalisation, including restoration, of individual buildings, housing renewal for priority areas, adaptive reuse of historic buildings for priority areas, focusing on social and economic regeneration to improve living conditions and standards.

The Old City of Jerusalem was inscribed on the World Heritage list in 1981. It was then listed as a "World Heritage site in danger" in 1982. The Old City is suffering from the deterioration of the social, economic and housing conditions of its Palestinian residents as well as the deterioration of the physical conditions of its buildings, monuments and utilities. On the other hand there is a systematic and organised campaign by some Israeli extreme groups for ethnic replacement of the Palestinian population by Jewish settlers. In addition to the political implication of these attempts, such actions are directly and indirectly threatening the cultural identity and architectural characteristics of the Old City and its cultural heritage.

The OCJRP tried to address these problems. A number of projects were selected under emergency and total restoration components according to special criteria. The criteria were developed after an extensive pilot survey for one of the most vulnerable areas in the Old City. This area, known as Aqabet al-Khaldyeh in the Islamic quarter close to al-Haram al-Sharif, suffers from economic and social deprivation. The findings of the physical, economic, demographic and social surveys in this area indicated the need to prepare a comprehensive plan for the revitalisation of the Old City. The plan is now completed and was published in Arabic in 2001 and in English in 2003. It is expected that the plan will create a scientific base for intervention and required action to improve the living conditions in the Old City, regenerate the economy, upgrade housing and services and protect the City's identity and heritage. The revitalisation plan will hopefully direct professionals and decision makers to jump start the redevelopment process in the Old City.

Through the survey and studies carried out while preparing the revitalisation plan and as a result of the experience accumulated from restoration and rehabilitation projects implemented in the Old City, the Technical Office developed better understanding of how the city works, and what are the main factors which may influence its future. Most importantly, the team became more involved with the community and local institutions who shared and assisted in the implementation process.

A community outreach programme funded since the year 2000 by the Ford Foundation established a much-needed link connecting the technical team with the end user, local institutions, and grassroots organisations in the Old City of Jerusalem. The programme created a platform for dialogue between the various actors and assisted in identifying priorities defining problems and subsequently overcoming them.

REVITALISE TO SURVIVE

The regeneration of inner cities and the revitalisation of historic centres recently became part of the overall urban development programme for towns, cities and urban centres. To achieve sustainability, planners should take into consideration the long term prospects and potential of the city, and that includes all its assets and cultural resources.

Consequently, revitalisation of these areas became an integrated part of the urban and economic development process. Therefore, a dynamic and progressive approach involving historic buildings and monuments is required to adapt them for modern uses and facilities while preserving their cultural value. To enable the inclusion of urban renewal within the urban planning of a city, special attention should be given to investigate, diagnose and analyse these areas before integrating them in the overall development plans for the 'modern' city.

To succeed in affecting a positive change in the life of residents in the Old City of Jerusalem while protecting its outstanding architectural heritage, a dynamic and flexible approach based on diverse and multi-disciplinary skills is required.

The Welfare Association is hoping to meet this challenge by continuously developing its programme and activities to respond to the urgent and growing needs of the city and its residents. Its mission in the Old City of Jerusalem with all its complexities is to preserve the monuments while protecting the human dignity of its residents and to revitalise this most valuable World Heritage city while restoring hope and faith to its community.

For illustrations of projects in Jerusalem, the reader is referred to pls. 36-41 and 91.

New Life for the Medina of Tunis

SÉMIA AKROUT-YAÏCHE

WHAT THE PROGRAMMES HAVE ACCOMPLISHED

Quite recently, the notion of the historical centre of a city has been superimposed on that of the historical monument. Today, the concept of valuing and protecting ancient city cores, together with the idea of heritage conservation, includes not just exceptional buildings, but also the contextual value of their location. In Tunisia today, heritage is no longer considered only as a cultural value, but also as a means towards progress and development.

It is not easy to protect sites that are steeped in culture and history and that are deeply rooted in the memory of the population, and to integrate them into a so-called 'modern' world, one that is mechanised and continually developing technically. Inspired by the examples of numerous other Mediterranean towns, Tunis has risen to this challenge. Tunis is without doubt one of the best-conserved Muslim Arab cities. With its twelve centuries of history, the Medina of Tunis contains numerous Islamic monuments: at the end of a street, one can discern the slim silhouette of a minaret or a dome covered with the green tiles of a *zawia*. Uninterrupted walls extend the length of even streets, where a nobleman's residence stands out with its rich stone surrounds and majestic nailed door.

A living testimony to Muslim urbanism, the residential areas of the Medina have remained relatively unchanged since the end of the eighteenth century. In 1979, UNESCO declared Tunis a World Heritage site. The town is characterised by its dense network of streets, alleys and cul-de-sacs leading to closely-knit patio houses. The architectural contribution of the 1850-1950 period is felt particularly in added apartment structures and official buildings that are situated on boulevards built on the site of the ancient city walls and in the suburbs. With its 270 hectares and more than one hundred thousand inhabitants, the Medina provides not only a record of the past, but also an immense developing area whose future forms an integral part of the main area of the Tunisian capital.

Since the 1960s, the Medina has attracted immigrants and travellers from rural areas, many of whom were ill-equipped for urban life, and this factor, amongst others, contributed to its decline: the decomposition of urban structures, deterioration of buildings (palaces and residences) and the decline of economic functions. It is important to study the course of action taken thus far, to examine both the positive and negative factors, in order to draw up solid future plans and programmes.

These actions will rapidly reach beyond the mandate of historical monuments to develop into proposals for integrated intervention and a protection policy based on two main themes.

Firstly, the protection of the monumental heritage in conjunction with the development of cultural tourism, this being a fundamental economic policy of Tunisia. Numerous monuments have been restored in recent years, the restorations have included mainly religious monuments (mosques, *zawias*, and so on), ancient Koranic schools (*madrasas*) and a few important residences, all of which reintegrated various collective enterprises (headquarters of associations, socio-cultural amenities, learning centres, and so on) which were capable of adapting and integrating into the structure without disfiguring it.

Secondly, the protection of the building heritage with social aims, amongst others, that of developing the socio-economic structure of a living Medina, fulfilling an important role in housing and craftsmanship of monuments. In recent years, considerable investment has been made in the infrastructure, amenities and housing in the Medina: the Hafsia project, financed partially by the World Bank in the scope of the third urban project; the Kasbah project with the construction of a large underground car park; and finally the sanitation project of the *oukalas* assisted by the Arab Fund for Social and Economic Development (FADES) and reinforced today by the construction of a new headquarters of the Town Hall in the centre of the Medina, set in a strategic and historic site of the Kasbah.

These projects have had an impact on the Medina, as much on the architectural, urban, social and economic fronts, as on its heritage plan. They have enabled entire zones to be selected under the improvement plan of the Medina as areas for restructuring due to their dilapidated state, and especially to develop directives for improving social housing, resulting in the creation of various financial, legislative and technical institutions, capable of intervening to resolve problems. They are conceived as integrated projects, bringing together several components such as renovation, rehabilitation, and improvement of infrastructures, together with the creation of employment.

Proof of the relevance and performance of these projects can be seen through the presence of the two international financial institutions, International Bank for Reconstruction and Development (BIRD) and FADES, who, for the first time in their history, provided financing for the housing rehabilitation project of a historic centre. A coherent approach to the restructuring project of the Hafsia area has succeeded in reversing the process of degradation which has been ongoing there since the beginning of the twentieth century, and has succeeded in improving the area's infrastructure while strengthening the traditional urban fabric of the Medina. This project, which has twice won the Aga Khan Award for Architecture, has also been successful in reviving commercial activities in the area, and it has replaced or restored some of the housing in ruins and encouraged communications between residents from different social classes.

The Oukalas project, partially financed by FADES, has contributed to the renaissance of the Medina. One notes with satisfaction the beginnings of a return to this historic town. The progress of this important national project has been followed closely by the President of the Republic since it began in 1990. It was created with the aim of accomplishing:

- the recovery of rental accommodations in a state of collapse. To this effect, more than 1300 households evacuated from 256 *oukalas* have been rehoused in three stages by the Municipality to the satellite cities created to accommodate them;
- 404 buildings (thirty of which belong to the Municipality and the State) are the object of the rehabilitation and restoration programme. A credit facility of fifteen million dinars has been allocated to owners for renovation of their buildings, with an interest rate of five percent and repayment over fifteen years.

Buildings which are of architectural and/or historical interest are proposed for restoration under a re-allocation programme run by cultural or social collectives.

PROPOSALS AND PERSPECTIVES

Following this assessment and report, consideration was given for the adoption of a new strategy in continuation, and complementary, to the ones already complete or in the process of completion, notably those projects of social interest, such as the Hafsia and *oukalas*.

The selected strategy relies mainly on the strengthening of the first concept presented, namely the preservation of monumental heritage, since we believe today that after having resolved the sanitation/decay problems and controlled the deterioration process we can gently modify our policies to extend to cultural entertainment, the improvement and reconciliation of this heritage with contemporary life. To achieve this, a two-point plan is proposed:

- first, adequate legislation regarding the classification of historic monuments and a protection plan;
- second, the recognition of the value of monumental heritage with respect to:
  - urban aesthetics;
  - the promotion of culture;
  - the promotion of cultural tourism;
  - economic promotion;
  - resolving traffic and parking problems.

The first concept poses no problems – new legislation is underway and a protection plan is being elaborated. The second concept, however, is more complex to develop, and requires an effort on the part of decision makers, adequate financing and expertise equal to the high level of expectations.

We are party, therefore, to a well-expressed desire on the part of the towns' leaders to link monumental heritage to urban development of the city. Several attempts have been made to transform buildings which until recently were in a state of ruin (religious buildings, *madrasas*, *fondouks* [market places], palaces and abandoned residences) into places of prestige, alive with art and culture and contributing to the socio-economic promotion of the city.

Consequently, we find ourselves surrounded by an important stock of monuments of architectural or historic interest, belonging to the State or the Municipality as a result of the Oukalas land and social rehabilitation project, and for which an adequate programme is essential.

OPERATIONAL APPROACH FOR THE CULTURAL AND ECONOMIC PROMOTION
OF THIS HERITAGE

The fundamental approach to appreciating this heritage is to restore it, and to follow a new relocation programme if the original function no longer exists. Conversion to another use enables a restored monument to survive and to play an important role in the development of a city. Interest in cultural tourism and the culture of the Medina has grown in recent years, and it has gradually become a favoured site in the Tunis area for ambitious cultural projects. Cultural hubs have begun to form around the restored areas. These are cultural areas but also attractive spaces capable of stimulating the creation of visitors' itineraries leading to the restored and reused monuments. This is particularly true in light of the trend for public amenities to return towards the heart of the old town (Festival de la Médina, Musée de la Ville, Musée de la Broderie).

It is important to encourage the development of refined tourist accommodation (elegant, privately-run hotels and luxury hotels), to avoid the Medina becoming merely a brief stopover point on the guided tour circuits. Some fifty monuments have been identified, indexed and studied. Concise project files have been drawn up for each building which detail their presentation, provide a diagnostic appraisal, record restoration work and also propose reallocation depending upon the site's capacity, its typology and its geographic position in relation to the cultural and tourist centres developing in the Medina and which need reinforcing.

This provides a brief outline of an urban development plan and attempts to describe the problems encountered during restoration/re-conversion, especially in the planning stages, an important period before any intervention. How can we rise to the double challenge of development and conversion? Planning is clearly of considerable importance in this process, and consideration needs to be given to the type of activity, the type of building and the choice of amenities to be housed within these historic sites. We hope to find solutions to all these questions by studying the different approaches and methods of similar cases experienced in other towns in the region.

For illustrations of projects in Tunis, the reader is referred to pls. 42-48.

The Heritage of Bukhara

NASSIM SHARIPOV AND SELMA AL-RADI

A famous Japanese humanist of the twentieth century said: "Nothing brings us as close to understanding other people as touching their cultural roots". Learning about and preserving the cultural heritage of Central Asian people is an enormous and highly important task. Over the centuries caravans of camels came out of China headed towards Europe, six thousand kilometres away. In spite of dangers, they went through the deserts, waterless steppes and mountain paths of Central Asia carrying all kind of goods – the most valuable and expensive being silk. Chinese masters kept the secret of producing silk carefully guarded. Because of it, the nineteenth-century German geographer and geologist, Ferdinand von Richthofen, called the caravan routes connecting the East and the West the "Silk Road". The Silk Road played a great role in the development of urban civilisation and in creating trade relations between the countries along its path.

Movement along the Silk Road was responsible for the creation of a distinctive and unique transcontinental culture. Famous architectural monuments, craft items of great masters, were not only important from an economic point of view, they also depicted the philosophy of striving to secure knowledge of the world, and of the culture of other nations. Bukhara, in Uzbekistan, is one of the most ancient cities in the world, and one of the most important cultural and economic centres on the Silk Road. For twenty-five centuries the city made a significant contribution to the development of material culture and was a mediator between East and West. Bukhara was a capital of a vast state and one of the important centres of the Muslim East. It is a homeland of great thinkers, poets and architects, such as Imam Al-Bukhari, Mohammed Narshaki, Daqiqi, Avicenna, Rudaki, Ahmad Danish, Abid, Sadriddin Aini and many others.

A dense pattern of low buildings creates an original composition that represents the background for the monuments and architectural complexes of the city. Narrow winding streets, which lead to the group of monuments, expose them in an unexpected way and create surprise at their scale and architecture. When one approaches the city from the northern or north-western gates the beautiful silhouette of ancient Bukhara is visible. Visitors call Bukhara a "museum under the open sky". With a population of no more than three hundred thousand people Bukhara boasts more than five hundred architectural monuments of different styles and schools. The monuments are preserved in their original context and are in harmony with the city's modern structure.

MAUSOLEUM OF THE SAMANIDS

Built in the ninth to tenth centuries on the orders of Ismail Samani, the great ruler and landowner of the Mavera-un-nahr lands, this mausoleum was erected as a family (dynasty) crypt. According to the rules of early Islam it was forbidden to build any kind of construction over a grave, but this rule was broken by caliphs from Bagdad in the middle of the ninth century. This mausoleum is very modest in size, but gives the impression of a monumental building, achieved through simplicity of forms, accuracy and decorative decoration. A cubic volume is set up on a square platform and crowned by a hemispherical dome, with four small oval cupolas at the corners, and an arched gallery. All its façades are identical.

KALYAN MINARET AND MOSQUE

This minaret is the main vertical element in the silhouette of Bukhara, visible from most of the city. Completed in 1127 it is forty-six metres high and is an example of near perfect engineering. The minaret is crowned by a sixteen-arched rotunda – up to which the muezzin climbed using a spiral staircase to call the people to prayer. There seems to have been one more conical element, but only a small part of it has been preserved. The twelfth-century mosque is located near the minaret, but it fell into decline during the Mongol invasion (pls. 49, 54, 55). In the fifteenth century restoration work was undertaken. At that time the majolica panel of the main building of the mosque – *maqsura* and *mihrab* – was laid out, and the name of the craftsman, Bayazid, survived. When the Uzbek dynasty of the Sheybanids came to power in the sixteenth century the mosque was radically rebuilt in 1514. The name of the mosque and the minaret is "Kalyan", which translates as "great" and relates to the size of the monuments.

MIR-I ARAB MADRASA

Located just opposite the Kalyan Mosque, this *madrasa* was built on the orders of the influential Sheikh Mir-i Arab and finished in 1535/1556 (pls. 51, 57). The building was erected on a high platform to elevate it above the square. The *madrasa* was built in a traditional composition and style. The architectural decor of the main and courtyard façades with carved and multicoloured mosaics is especially beautiful. Geometrical and tiny stylised floral ornament, and refined inscriptions (*suls*) with intricate interweaving of words are distributed on the wall, arches and other parts of the building.

MAGAK-I ATTAR MOSQUE

Built on the site of a pre-Islamic temple, the name of this mosque includes the ancient word "Mag" (Zoroaster priest) or "Mogh" (the god of the Moon). Archaeological work shows that during the Samanid period a mosque was erected here, but in the twelfth century it was rebuilt. The level of the floor was raised and the main façade was decorated then. In the sixteenth century the mosque was again rebuilt and was partially buried underground, since the level of the streets rose. In the twentieth century the main façade was cleaned up to 4.5 metres, explaining its present appearance. The Magak-i Attar Mosque is a unique example of the architecture of Central Asia during the Karakhanid dynasty.

CHASHMA AYUB

This monument is called a mausoleum, but it is not one. According to legend, Ayub, or the Biblical figure Job, came to this waterless area. He struck his staff on the ground and a well (*chashma*) of water appeared. The water was considered medicinal. The reverence of Job is of course connected with the pre-Islamic period and the cult of water. The building was erected in 1390 during the rule of Timur.

MADRASA OF ULUGH BEG

Ulugh Beg was a grandson of Tamerlane, who ruled from 1409 to 1449. Known as a scientist and patron of sciences, he erected several *madrasas* in various cities, the first of these in 1415 in Bukhara. It has modest dimensions, but the style is harmonious and characteristic of the architecture of the Timurid Renaissance. The name of the architect is known – Ismail bin Tahir bin Mahmud Isfahani – the descendant of a master brought from Iran by Tamerlane.

Much of the architecture linked to trade along the Silk Road survives in Bukhara. The Taqi-Zargaran – or "Jewellers Dome" – is located near Poi-Kalon Square. It was mentioned in the beginning of the sixteenth century and was obviously erected in the time of the Timurids with further transformation in the reign of Abdullah Khan. It was built at the intersection of two streets, its entrances outlined with arched portals. The huge dome rises above the inner space surrounded by more than thirty trade and craft stalls under the smaller cupolas, where jewellery was produced and sold. Further along in the same market area the Tim of Abdullah Khan is located. It is a trade construction for the sale of silk, its closed square space covered with domes. The central dome is particularly present and there are galleries around it, covered by many smaller domes. The arched niches divide the space into fifty-eight separate stalls. Another significant commercial structure is the Taqi-Telpak Forushon – "The Cupola of the Headdress Sellers". The architect of this structure had the difficult task of erecting it on the intersection of several streets at random angles. The building is crowned by a cupola with a row of windows at its base, giving uniform light. This complex leads to the Taqi-Sarrafan – or "Money Changers Dome". The central dome is based on four strong intersecting arches, which are visible outside showing its engineering. The shops of the money changers, who played a great role in the trading life of Bukhara, were below it.

In the eighteenth century, Central Asia faced social and economic decline and construction of monuments came to a halt. In 1712, just opposite the fortress, a mosque was nonetheless built which was finished at the beginning of the twentieth century. In front of the mosque there is a water reservoir which gave its name to the whole complex, Bala Hauz. In 1917 a famous Bukhara craftsman, Usta Shirin Muradov, erected a small minaret here which is a copy of the Kalyan Minaret.

In 1807 Khalif Niyazkul, a rich Turkmen, built the small Char-Minar *madrasa* (pl. 56) to the west of the Ulugh Beg *madrasa* and the *madrasa* of Abdul-Aziz Khan (pls. 52, 53). The architecture of this monument differs from the traditional style. There is a small courtyard with a pond covered by stone. The palace of the last ruler of Bukhara lies outside the city. There are in fact two palaces, one built at the end of the nineteenth century and the other in 1912-1914. The architecture of the palace is a mixture of European and Asian architectural forms. The old palace was built by the craftsman Khodzha Gaflı, and the new one by Abid Rahim Khaitov with the participation of two Russian engineers Sakovich and Margulis.

The Restoration of the Old City of Bukhara

Bukhara is located five hundred kilometres south-west of Tashkent and two hundred kilometres west of Samarkand. Founded in the middle of the first millennium BC, Bukhara became an important commercial, artistic and intellectual centre after its conquest by the Arabs in 709 AD. Destroyed by Genghis Khan in 1226, the importance of the city decreased in proportion to that of the Silk Road after reviving in the sixteenth century. An independent emirate from 1753 to 1868, it was then incorporated as a vassal state by Tsarist Russia. Bolshevik forces took Bukhara after the First World War and a number of its monuments suffered damage at that time. Uzbekistan declared its independence in 1990 and Bukhara became a provincial capital. Situated on the edge of the Kizilkum desert, the city has an arid climate and is mainly made of low-rise brick structures. The Soviet-era new city surrounds the old with a ring of concrete high-rises. A restoration programme for the old city was begun by the USSR in the 1970s, in the hope of developing tourism. The Institute of Restoration of the Ministry of Culture in Tashkent undertook research work on the history of significant monuments and made up detailed drawings and project outlines for each one. Aside from restoration, buildings had basic utilities added, but no new additions were permitted. Since there were few practicing Muslims after fifty years of Soviet rule, new 'politically correct' functions had to be found for most of the structures.

997 historical monuments were identified in the immediate region of Bukhara, of which some five hundred were located within the walls of the town. These included twenty-four *madrasas*, forty-eight mosques, fourteen caravanserais, nine mausoleums, eight archaeological sites and 265 hous-

es. The majority of these monuments are concentrated in the town centre. A 'passport' including plans and elevations, old photos, a description of its physical state, and its restoration history was made up for each of these identified locations. Restoration efforts concentrated on the major monuments and a number of modern eyesores were razed, creating open spaces that permit better viewing of the historical buildings. Great care was taken to reconstitute the original decor wherever possible, including glazed tiles, paintings or carved bricks. Prior to a 1976 earthquake, only traditional materials were used in restoration work, but new regulations after that date required the use of reinforced concrete for load-bearing walls and portals. A gradual return to traditional materials was made thereafter, however.

A large number of architects worked on the monuments of Bukhara, all employees of the Institute of Restoration in Tashkent. The Ministry of Culture in Tashkent supplied contractors, engineers and other specialists, and very little use was made of foreign consultants. The restoration work in Bukhara, which in fact began as early as the 1920s after the Bolshevik bombardments, has continued since the fall of the Soviet Union. In 1996, there were forty restoration projects underway or planned in the city. Although private donations are made, they usually amount to no more than one percent of the budget for the renovations. The labour force employed on these projects is local, with the specialised craftsmen, or *ustas*, usually belonging to a family with a long history in that craft.

The old town of Bukhara functions well. It is used continuously by the people who live in the immediate vicinity as well as by the more general population. Sunday bazaars draw crowds of thousands of people, and it can be said that on the whole the restoration efforts have been highly successful. One threat to the historic monuments of the city is the rising level of saline ground water that has infiltrated and damaged many walls. A large number of monuments in Bukhara is covered with a film of salt along their lower walls and very few trees can survive given the salinity of this ground water. Although technical solutions have been proposed to ease this difficulty, their cost is such that the Uzbek government has not been able to finance them.

As a whole, the combination of community effort and technical expertise represented in this project deserves high praise. The civic pride and enhanced cultural identity that are the outgrowth of this work demonstrate that a legacy can be more than a museum or a tourist destination. It can become an important part of the living present, to be used and enjoyed by residents and visitors alike; a continuing inspiration for new architecture and urbanism.

This text was adapted from a Technical Review Summary presented to the Aga Khan Award for Architecture in 1995 by Selma al-Radi.

For illustrations of Bukhara, the reader is referred to pls. 49-57.

Building in the Persian Gulf

NADER ARDALAN

My four decades of professional and academic life have been, more or less, equally spent in three geographic-cultural zones of concentration: Iran, North America and the Persian Gulf States, with project excursions, of course, to the Far East, Central and Western Europe and North Africa.

With regard to the seminar theme of "Architecture for Changing Societies", I shall illustrate my contribution with a brief series of case studies and findings on this topic from the years of my most recent works in the Persian Gulf States of Kuwait, Saudi Arabia, Qatar and the United Arab Emirates.

The specific focus will be the subject of 'identity' — with the sub topics of unity within the diversity of image identities that our clients and users of the projects have sought through us, as their self-expressions and their most cherished visions for their future. In this latter context, we have been the passive receivers of their hopes and dreams.

Ever since the research and publication of a seminal work that I co-authored, entitled *The Sense of Unity* (1973), which interestingly enough has just recently been published in its Farsi translation and sponsored by the Municipality of Tehran, my design work has been structured upon the key principles of functional purpose, environmental adaptation and cultural relevance.

Functional purpose relates to the project use and its functional and measurable needs. It also includes project feasibility as related to time, economics, implementation, maintenance and operation of the buildings produced. Often architects and clients are satisfied with these criteria of design alone, but this would lack context and the quality of a 'soul' for the architecture.

Environmental adaptation is dedication to sustainable design principles. These principles provoke the correct bio-climatic orientation of building forms in space with respect to sun, wind, terrain and view. They generate optimum site planning strategies with an emphasis on adaptive landscaping and interior architectural strategies are inspired that support a 'green', energy-efficient architecture. The dramatic and innovative use of technology and construction materials to achieve energy-efficient designs complement and complete these criteria of design.

Cultural relevance is the accommodation of indigenous socio-cultural patterns and the human condition in architecture. It concerns the correct integration and exaltation of the signs and symbols of specific cultural identity re-affirmations of society that have accrued through the ages. Finally it touches the immeasurable, higher quests of self-actualisation, based upon the most profound archetypal perceptions of that society and the cultural intellectual paradigms of the times.

In many ways, Charles Jencks was addressing this aspect of design when he spoke of the "new paradigm in architecture", with particular reference to his concept of the "enigmatic signifier".

THE DIVERSITY OF IMAGE IDENTITY

We have observed two polar tendencies with regard to image identity that have most influenced the design and character of our projects in the Persian Gulf states over the last decade or so. At one extreme there are those clients who seek traditional images and environments, while at the other there are those who seek a totally international image. Naturally, in between the two a wide range exists, but at their fulcrum there has been the opportunity to explore the new integration – the "Khalq-i Jadid" or the New Creation, which is a sensitive and balanced fusion of the two polar dimensions.

TRADITIONAL / REGIONAL IDENTITY

I first researched and design explored the traditions in the architecture of the Middle East in Iran in the late 1960s and 1970s. Examples of this work are the Iran Centre for Management Studies with Harvard University built in 1972, which today is named Imam Sadegh University (pl. 26). It was based upon the concept of the classic Persian Garden, such as the Bagh-i-Fin in Kashan and the *madrasa* courtyard plan. Built in simple load-bearing brick, the project inspired other Iranian colleagues of that time to also explore the traditional regional vocabulary of signs, symbols, metaphors and construction methods of post tenth-century Seljuk brick architecture.

With regard to the Persian Gulf and the Arabian Peninsula, I first became familiar with this region as a result of a commission in the early 1970s to document, research and write the completion report of the new Masjid-i-Haram and the history of the Holy Kaaba in Mecca. This book was published by the Ministry of Finance of Saudi Arabia. This experience left a profound impact.

My understanding of Persian Gulf architecture has been greatly enhanced since moving to Kuwait in 1994 to direct the design of KEO International, a 500 staff multi-disciplinary firm with branch offices in Qatar, the UAE, Lebanon and Washington DC.

A case in point is the Souk al-Sharq on the waterfront of Kuwait completed by us in 1998 (pl. 62). The former Mayor of Kuwait asked for this major downtown waterfront project to provide a regional image and environment to a city that had in the 1960s and 1970s completely demolished almost all of its traditional urban fabric of courtyard houses.

After a survey of the old souk of Kuwait, which is one of the few traditional urban environments remaining in Kuwait, and a historical-visual site analysis of the 2.7-kilometre waterfront site, we designed a 76,000 square-metre shopping mall in the form of a great souk or bazaar, a fish market and boat harbour by the sea.

Much of the indigenous architecture of Kuwait and other emirates has been historically influenced by their Iranian neighbours across the Gulf in Bandar-e Bushehr, Bandar Lengeh and other Persian ports. Another contributing factor has been that Iranian architects and masons were used in designing and building many of their landmark historic buildings. Thus it was natural that we developed our design on traditional Persian Gulf forms based upon the linear order of a compact bazaar with gateways, *badgirs* (which integrated contemporary heating, ventilation and air conditioning systems in their form), and constructed the whole ensemble in buff, brick and stone cladding to a reinforced concrete structure. This bazaar, or souk, form was set upon a man-made island dredged from the Gulf waters that helped create boat harbours for both the fishing fleet of Kuwait and public pleasure boating. The Souk al-Sharq waterfront project has become a socially lively and economically successful place for Kuwait with a distinctive traditional regional image. *Architectural Review* published the work in their spring 2000 edition on the Middle East.

Other traditional image projects have included the Kuwait Sheraton Diamond Ballroom. The ceiling design was based upon the geometric diminution of the square root of two rotations, while the great carpet was based upon the pattern of the famous 'Ardabil' carpet in the Victoria and Albert Museum in London, which was transformed by computer stylisation.

Finally a series of buff, brick residential courtyard houses and apartments have been designed and built in Kuwait that have been traditionally inspired, yet some have even reached heights of twenty storeys.

The lessons from the above case studies demonstrate that both senior municipal clients, major real estate developers and private home owners have genuine tendencies to seek a traditional, historic image identity for their building designs. Yet these forms and images do not just simply replicate past styles, rather they exhibit a high level of sophistication in researching the spirit of regional forms for their valuable lessons in environmentally adaptive design and perennial culturally vital symbols.

This climatically and culturally sensitive design approach has motivated other noted architects such as Hassan Fathy, Abdul Wahed El-Wakil in Egypt, Mohammed Makiya in Iraq, Mazhur Islam in Bangladesh and Kamran Diba in Iran.

CONTEMPORARY INTERNATIONAL IDENTITY
What could be more international and high-tech than a car showroom for Mercedes Benz? Multi-national companies and global enterprises often come with their own branding and image identity that is paramount for their international marketing continuity.

In the case related to the new Mercedes Benz showroom in Kuwait, we were actually inspired by the three pointed star of the Benz logo, which formed the structural steel expression of the main circular roof of the project (pl. 58). This innovative design concept had not previously been used in any Mercedes showroom, yet clearly worked within the framework of the branding concept of this corporation and the corner site selected for the project location.

The epitome of the international image quest came in the shape of a forty-storey office tower that we were commissioned to design for the Al Shaya Group in Kuwait. The programme brief asked for a state-of-the-art speculative office building that was 'IT smart' with a raised floor design, and fully flexible to accommodate an international business centre. The Nautilus, as we named the project design, was once again inspired by the proximity of the project to the Persian Gulf and the needs of correct adaptive environmental design and the functional necessities of a modern office tower.

The lessons here are that globalisation carries with it international images. These images deal with market forces of product branding, high-tech building systems and materials and a modern identity, in which the priorities of decision making place a higher value on functional purpose, technical innovation and climatic adaptation than on regional cultural relevance. For these reasons they appear as dynamic aberrations in the context of their Persian Gulf context. They pose as many questions as they provide solutions. Yet they are the problematic precursors of the inevitable change that is sweeping the region.

Are they the new architectural paradigms or only intermediary ones, leading to yet new, more culturally and environmentally more relevant solutions of greater and longer duration of both social and aesthetic value?

NEW INTEGRATION
In my own personal search for more meaningful holistic designs that can lead to more relevant and innovative architectural paradigms for the Persian Gulf, three projects come to the forefront.

The first is the Oil Company headquarters for the ADMA-OPCO and ADGAS companies that was completed in 1995 on the corniche of Abu Dhabi, UAE. This project was won in a world design competition in 1990 while design partner of another firm in Boston, and in joint venture with Ove Arup and Partners.

The design sought a 'timeless grace' for the architecture for one of the institutions of this country. Both artistically and authoritatively it reinterpreted the traditions of this ancient land, drawing on its inexhaustible fountainhead of archetypal imagery, metaphors and symbols to preserve a cumulative memory for the future. Yet it is thoroughly modern, incorporating state-of-the-art building systems, efficient and flexible office planning strategies and one of the world's tallest vertical gardens protected by a twenty-storey clear glass atrium facing north towards the Persian Gulf waters.

Before the design ever began, the design team researched the archaeological history of the UAE, visited the ethnographic museums of the country and recorded the cultural artefacts of the place for indigenous patterns and forms. We researched the regional system of irrigation of the date palm oasis that characterises the country and interviewed the users to understand their cultural and social patterns of space usage and daily activities. The culmination of these research studies provided the design and client team with a sense of a 'higher' purpose in the conception and construction of the headquarters.

In another, more recent invited international design competition for the Information Technology College of the UAE University in Al Ain, our entry was awarded first prize. The project is about to commence construction. Charles Jencks has written: "This dynamic world view, just dawning, asks us to consider the idea that the Universe is a single, unfolding self-organising event, something more biological and anatomical than machine, something radically interconnected and creative, an entity that jumps suddenly to higher levels of organisation and order that delights us as it does so."

A new architectural paradigm has emerged to meet the innovative challenges of the IT College programme and the more generalised new consciousness that characterises the third millennium we have just entered.

This reaffirmation of order in the universe and the interconnectedness of all existence is an eternal message of faith and a vital new inspiration wishing to be expressed in architecture, especially in Islamic cultures so rooted in faith and with such an illustrious architectural heritage.

Translating this vision into architecture presents some difficulties, but that has always been the challenge at such historic thresholds. The choice of an appropriate visual model or paradigm to represent the new global, scientific, philosophic, or spiritual consciousness can however be metamorphic.

There are different models, which have been proposed by leading thinkers that lend themselves to appropriate interpretation. For instance, the model can be set out with a geometric order, in the form of a flower, a rotating spiral, as fractals, waves or billowing clouds. The visual impulse is towards a dynamic unfolding image that has a sense of inherent order and transcendence.

Micro inspection of the functional necessity of an IT centre in Al Ain complements this macro view of paradigm form selection. Research has shown that its guest form is to be compact around a central core, transparent and sustainable.

The cumulative micro/macro resolution proposed as the optimum form of the IT College then emerged as a compact elliptical volume, shaped as a rotating spiral set on the site with a solar orientation of its long axis tilted slightly to the south-east, traversed by an east-west circulation axis that related it directly to its university context of buildings and the gender separated movement systems.

The last project in this series of the new integration theme is the Al Ain Diwan which shall serve as the new Governor's headquarters for this garden city in the UAE (pl. 60). The design vision established the theme of a dialogue between the 'ruler and the community'. It was agreed with the client that this sense of a place of dialogue could be most effectively accomplished through the periodic recapitulation of the essential mythologies of the community. The noted cultural anthropologist, Joseph Campbell, wrote: "Myths are so intimately bound to culture, time and place that unless symbols and metaphors are kept alive by constant recreation through the arts (and architecture), life just slips away from them".

It was decided that the Diwan was to be the place where these mythologies and epic fables could be discreetly and elegantly displayed in the very form of the building, in its plan and in the visual images of the main spaces, plus the very materials from which the building and space are made.

CONCLUDING OBSERVATIONS
Just walking down a street in downtown Kuwait or any of the Persian Gulf city states, one is amazed by the variety of the modes of attire of the populace. There are traditional women covered completely in black from head to toe, with full cover black veils and gloves, even in the heat of summer. Accompanying them and walking a few steps ahead may be men whose tendencies to extreme traditionalist belief is revealed by the length of their dishdash, the cut and the length of their beards and the particularities or lack of an *aghl*.

Contrasting in their mode of attire to the above, on the very same street, are also local citizens in totally western garb, women with flowing, coiffured hair driving the latest model cars with one hand on the wheel and the other holding fast to a mobile phone.

Demographically, too, the Persian Gulf states are very diverse in the proportion of nationals to expatriates (as non-citizens are referred to). Dubai is said to have less than twenty percent nationals resident in the city, while Bahrain is in the vast majority composed of national citizens. This demographic diversity also has an impact on the issue of cultural identity. For instance, in Dubai, some architects have asked: "Whose identity are we going to address? Will it be that of the minority nationals or of the vast majority of internationals?" And the cityscape shows this diversity very graphically.

These are civilisations in transition and we, as architects, build the containers for these social groupings that are transforming. Within this context, it is becoming more important than ever that architects think about their work in view of its ethical ramifications. In addition to meeting the individual client's desires, we must protect the public's health, safety and welfare and truly serve the higher values of society. This service to society requires that in whatever we do, the first rule must be to protect the environment and design sustainable architecture. The identity issue related to cultural-social relevance will require a great diversity of expression accommodating and reflecting this social diversity. Thus the architect in such societies of dynamic change needs to be deeply knowledgeable of a wide range of architectural expressions, yet possessing an inner core vision of profound meanings to guide his decision making.

However, regardless of the identity image issue, the architect needs to be courageous and innovative enough to cultivate the Aristotelian 'golden mean', to find the perfect balance between the past and the aspirations towards the future. In this quest the world of archetypal paradigms, the perennial metaphors of civilisations can be a guiding light. Louis Kahn said in Isfahan in 1970: "Traditions are as golden dust falling in space. If one but had the possibility of grasping this golden dust, we would possess the powers of anticipation of the future."

For projects by Nader Ardalan, the reader is referred to pls. 26 and 58-64.

Turkey Between East and West

AYDAN BALAMIR

INTRODUCTION: THE QUESTION OF IDENTITY AND CULTURAL INCERTITUDE

This paper intends to propose an overview of modern architecture in Turkey. Examples will include as much ordinary buildings as emblematic ones, taking the liberty of stretching the scope as far back to the 1920s, so as to touch on the experience of Modernism in Turkey. The central theme that binds all issues and examples to be covered will be the question of identity that the Turkish architect has encountered since the foundation of the Republic in 1923.[1]

Contemporary Turkish architecture, as I portray it, has suffered from a sense of hesitancy regarding cultural identity. Throughout the Republican period, the question of identity continued to revolve around dualities such as East-West, religious-secular, national-universal, and so on. Caught within a problem of tradition versus modernity, the subject occupied political and cultural agendas alike. Geographically situated between the Orient and the Occident, historically confused between loyalty preferences for Asiatic, Anatolian, Ottoman and Early Republican heritages, the in-between nature of Turkey has always been a source of many forms of hesitancy. Stylistic debates in architecture have followed the same line of argument, leading to identity exercises along cultural polarities.

This hesitancy, or incertitude as to the question of identity, has been the source of many problems in Turkey. Many projects have been undermined by this habit; but it has been a source of cultural wealth as well. If Turkey has survived so many problems, it was partly because of its relative openness to review, time and again, the identity it has taken up. One may view this also as a sign of Turkey's assimilation of Modernism, despite all the flaws and shortcomings in its application. A quote from the domain of cultural studies would be relevant to argue for the positive side of this incertitude concerning identity. Incertitude is regarded as "symptomatic of the modern consciousness, to the extent of anxiety", as Kellner summarises, "...for one is never certain that one has made the right choice, that one has chosen one's 'true' identity, or even constituted an identity at all. The modern self is aware of the constructed nature of identity and that one can always change and modify one's identity at will. One is also anxious concerning recognition and validation of one's identity by others."[2]

It is possible to produce evidence, in all aspects of political and cultural life, that reveals persistent anxiety concerning the nation's taking up of the right identity as well as its recognition by the West.

The project of westernisation has been taken at times rather literally, moulding its aspirations into the model of the French, German, American or Japanese, as the case may be. The habit of following patterns elsewhere is observed by the challengers of westernisation alike, growing aspiration towards Saudi or Farsi sources of inspiration. Architecture and city building constitute one appropriate context to discuss the experience of westernisation and its alternatives in Turkey – a context which offers many tangible forms and cases for a critical rethinking of the modernisation project, its post-modern phase and the current situation.

EARLY REPUBLICAN INCERTITUDE:
BETWEEN EUROPEAN MODERNISM AND NATIONALIST CURRENTS

The Turkish Hearth Society (pl. 65) and Ministry of National Defence, two buildings from 1927, present a perfect pair to express the cultural hesitancy during the founding years of the Republic. The one with Neo-Ottoman features embodied the nationalist currents from the turn of the century, termed later as the "1st National Style"; the other with plain features, the so-called "cubic architecture" brought in by Austrian architects, was fairly new for the country. The barren landscape of Ankara, the newly emerging capital of the Republic, offered examples of both ideas, representing in their confident gestures two identities that the Republic oscillated between: being heir to the Ottoman heritage and total denial of it.

The founding fathers of the Republic found in modern architecture a fellowship of spirit. It suited the progressive ideals of the new nation, which was geared to a radical project of 'civilisation change' in the direction of the West. Initially however, during the first attempts at westernisation during the late Ottoman era, the nationalist thesis was that the new Turkish identity would mediate between foreign and native resources, 'taming' western civilisation with elements of eastern culture. Marked with the opposition of 'universal civilisation' and 'national cultures' the underlying nationalist aspirations of the thesis were not favoured by the founders of the Republic. The building of a new capital provided every opportunity to launch the intended civilisation change, indicating directions to complement appearances, even more so perhaps than the case of specifying modern garments. Urban villas and multi-storey tenements in modern vocabularies brought a new culture of building and living in western ways. The locus of the 'West' was still Europe, though the French model was replaced with that of Austria and Germany, allies in the First World War.

With the excitement of a new architecture in keeping with the new ideals, a young generation of architects grew sceptical towards history and tradition. If a building were to resemble anything, it would not be the Ottoman style, because of its regressive connotations. The growing nationalist wave in the world during the 1940s, however, brought a rupture in the radical Modernism of the earlier years. The transformation of the Exhibition House built in 1933 into an Opera House in the 1940s is a bitter case in point where identity politics were exercised on a single building (pl. 66).

The new nationalist wave turned into two forms of regionalism under the leadership of Bruno Taut and Sedad Hakkı Eldem. While the former was characterised by the insertion of regional motifs in detail and ornament, the latter was codified in mass and façade composition, characterised by projecting eaves, oriels and fixed window proportions. Termed later as the "2nd National Style", Eldem's was an appropriation of the Anatolian vernacular – a source of inspiration that would revive time and again in the coming years. His recourse to tradition was far from being the sign of a reactionary inclination, given his justification of his architecture with the canons of architectural Modernism: the traditional timber house with its lightness of structure, demountable construction system and façades having numerous windows generously day-lighting the rooms, was in fact in line with the ideals of the Modern Movement.[3] Nevertheless, his emblematic Coffee House (pl. 69) was seldom approved by the architectural establishment, much attacked for its direct resemblance to a seventeenth-century mansion in the Bosphorus.

REPUBLICAN IDEALS 'UNDER BALANCE': AMERICAN MODERNISM, PRAGMATISM AND FAITH

A caricature in the 'Fine Arts Ball Gazette' of 1952 (pl. 67) is telling of the consecutive stages Turkish architecture underwent every ten years since the foundation of the Republic: Neo-Ottoman, European avant-garde, Neo-Vernacular, and finally American Modernism. The 1950s presented a clear 'Americanisation' in building and life culture, parallel to the shift in the conception of the 'West' in society. The flow of foreign aid from the USA to Turkey at the time, and the accompanying aspiration to become 'the little America' determined the new direction of identity and its architecture.

When Sedad Eldem collaborated with SOM for the Istanbul Hilton (pl. 70) in the International Style, his opponents accused him of an "identity twist."[4] The Hilton is known to be a turning point in modern Turkish architecture; buildings for tourism, business and commerce, would soon begin to emulate the vocabulary of American high Modernism. The implications of the Hilton have surpassed its architectural meaning, as one may perceive from passages that appeared in a 1955 issue of *Architectural Forum*: "High above the minarets of the Ottoman Empire, modern Turkey builds a symbol of progress, a focus of entertaining, and a magnet for the tourist trade... To many Turks, who long ago discarded the fez and the veil in favour of western ways, the new Istanbul Hilton symbolises something else: the hope that Turkey, once called the 'sick man of Europe', will become a healthy, wealthy and much visited member of the international family."[5]

The first multi-party election in 1950 was followed by a rupture from Early Republican ideals in many respects. The pro-American government opened the course of liberal economy, and started urban renewal projects shaped by sheer pragmatism. The passage to a multi-party regime also prompted a retrieval of dormant religious activism. The spread of the American lifestyle via movies, advertising and the physical environment to suit, paralleled the outspoken demands of religious groups for Islamic training and mosque building programmes, which had seen a pause in previous decades. The design and programming of mosques have involved, more than any other building type, agendas concerning the nation's integration with either the West or the East. Public disputes on mosque form became instances of broader political disputes about loyalty to Republican secularism or to political Islam. Architects' choices of modern or traditional forms began to be coded as messages of commitment to one or the other political stand.

The first military coup in 1960 ended with a new constitution with expanded democratic rights; the following decade saw the advent of left-wing social discourse rather than religious activism. Small-scale mosques dating from the 1960s illustrate the search for reconciliation between the principles of modern architecture and the traditional mosque image. The introduction of novelties did not create controversy among believers, unless the subject was distortedly propagated for political expediency. Kocatepe Mosque in Ankara was a monumental example, which would occupy the public agenda from 1957 onwards, until its completion in 1987. The prevention of the prize-winning project for the initial Kocatepe Mosque was due to political exploitation of the subject. The project was turned down for its modest size and novelty of form; the foundations were torn down in 1964, and a new competition was held, resulting in replication of a sixteenth-century Ottoman imperial mosque.

TRADITION AND MODERNISM DISSOLVE INTO SQUATTER TOWNS AND APARTMENT CITIES
For the architectural establishment of the 1950s and 1960s, traditional motifs were permissible only in stylised forms. Regionalist works ceased until their mass revival in the 1980s; Eldem's practice for Bosphorus mansions was among a handful of exceptions. The architects worked within the discipline of imported movements, particularly of the International Style, mastering its codes and craft at a time when the possibilities of the building industry in the country were very limited. Refined examples of international Modernism, produced with customised fixtures, furniture and carpentry, often with the paradigmatic 'bris soleil', were produced with very scarce means (pl. 68).

The 1950s saw the slab and point block constructions introduced in planned residential quarters. Decent products realised under CIAM principles attained a level of quality close to western examples. The cities were not shaped, however, by distinguished examples of the modernist craft. Migration to towns, housing shortage, and lack of a sufficient accumulation of capital gave way to a rapid urbanism that operated with relentless pragmatism and speculative interests. The growth of 'squatter towns' on the fringes paralleled the emergence of multi-storey 'apartment cities', having basically two variants: standardised blocks on narrow lots (built individually), or bundles of slab or point blocks (mostly mass produced) in formless agglomerations.

The invention of a modern vernacular altered the architectural landscape of Turkey, either eroding or totally erasing the traditional and early modern heritages alike. Characterised by a total disregard to varying contexts, the practice reproduced itself in every settlement, irrespective of its particularities. The majority of cities in Anatolia lost their historical fabric in just fifty years. They could not survive the greed for maximisation of urban rents. The demolition of historical quarters of towns to open wide traffic arteries or to provide several more storeys for developers resulted in reckless and ruthless transformation of urban land. A country which managed to save its cities from devastation by the bombs of the Second World War then self-destroyed its historical towns. Not only the house traditions of centuries, but also the earlier examples of modern housing have been gradually replaced by a deplorable practice, giving way to a complete break with an entire culture of dwelling and city building.

In a few decades, architects witnessed the divorce of building production from architecture and town planning, with a further divorce of architecture itself from town planning. Ironically, planning discipline was introduced to the State from the 1960s onwards, and independent city planning departments were established within architecture schools. Scholarly work done on squatter and vernacular settlements proliferated. While the study of the vernacular became institutionalised in the academia, the practice of high Modernism was vernacularised.

MODERNISM VERNACULARISED AND VULGARISED:
CONTRACTOR- AND MINISTRY-STYLED MODERNISM

The mainstream architectural production showed consistent decline in quality from the 1970s onwards. Increasingly, the contractor-dominated market of apartment flats for anonymous owners required no architectural talents, except for signature procedures. In the hands of lesser – if not totally fictitious – architects, a 'contractor modernism' emerged in its most prosaic forms. These apartment buildings are 'modern' only to the extent that they are reproductions of a reduced 'Domino frame', excluding its endless possibilities in free plan, as well as in massing. The design of apartment buildings turned into a restricted exercise in producing the most efficient plan and mass, to bring maximum profit to the contractor.

A rival in monotony and mediocrity to the contractor's modernism in apartment buildings was the technocrat's modernism in buildings for public services shaped by Ministry codes. A new generation of architects rose within state competitions held with official restrictions of the Ministry of Public Works. The Ministry's responsibility for the development and prosperity of the country bitterly conflicted with the resulting tectonic poverty in the built environment.

Within the architectural establishment, complete solidarity with the tenets of architectural Modernism continued until the mid-1970s. Distinguished architects of the late 1960s and 1970s turned from the International Style to variations on Organic Architecture and New Brutalism. The formal articulations of both soon surrendered to the mainstream paradigm, through applications of several formulae: fragmenting bulky forms into smaller scale masses and subdividing façades with numerous mullions to reveal the modular order. Sedad Eldem's Social Insurance Institution embodying such formulae was the model for many buildings for decades to come. Exemplary buildings were codified into a mediocre practice, vulgarised under Ministry codes and perpetuated through building production by public tender.

The mainstream practice of technocratic modernism grew violent from the 1970s onwards. Two consecutive *coup d'etats* took place in 1971 and 1980; expansion of the State during the military regimes gave way to governmental office buildings of colossal size. The modern language was neo-classicised to oppressive extremes; civic buildings, which are expected to be open and accessible for everyone, were inversely built in a temple monumentality and private estate seclusion. The professional and academic establishment was drained of its artistic roots, conducting an enterprise based on sheer instrumental rationality.

POST-MODERN 'LIBERATION': VARIATIONS ON THE STEREOTYPE

If the Post-Modern current had not emerged in the West, Turkish architects would have invented it. The stereotypes of contractor's and technocrat's modernism had taken much of the joy out of architecture. The growing awareness of the Turkish architect to the problem of identity was intensified by tedious repetitions of this mainstream practice, which was unjustly equated with genuine architectural Modernism.

During the 1980s, architectural Modernism became the scapegoat; the problem began to be voiced on all occasions, catchwords being "loss" or "lack" of identity. Two kinds of concern were discernable from discussions of identity in Turkish architecture.[6] The first was concerned with the absence of an identifiable 'Turkish character' in new buildings and towns; the second regarded the absence of any character at all, its cultural locus being less of a concern. Both views focused on 'distinctions' or 'distinguishable traits' as the terms identity and character imply, and they shared in common a concern with the presence of 'style' as an architectural response to the broader question of cultural identity. They varied, however, in their conception of cultural identity. Identity discussions of the first category were based on the assumption of an immutable identity: with varying emphases on regionalist, nationalist or religious lines of argument, they were inclined to see the cultural forms of the past as models to follow. The second group of discussions was open to embracing new identities, pointing to quality and character as end values.

With the delayed infiltration of the Post-Modernist discourse and language in the 1980s, stylish vocabularies began to be favoured. The most persistent ones up to today were the codifiable styles of Mario Botta and Hans Hollein; their formal gestures were among the first to be appropriated, to replace the crude vocabulary of the Ministry. Apartment blocks were to celebrate a greater stylistic freedom. Architects and developers, after years of asceticism, indulged in identity exercises along all sources of inspiration: Ottoman and Classical were among the favourites. However, since the exercise was confined to façade treatments of what is essentially the same apartment typology, this false liberation did not account for any recovery of an identifiable urban or house form. Nor did any identity politics lurk behind it; contrary to previous ideological loadings of architectural styles, the 'traditionalist' and 'modernist' appearance of new apartment buildings were often co-incidental or representative of taste cultures, without reference to any ideological stands of developers or inhabitants.

On the other hand, mosque building began to be invariably realised in traditional guises. Architects were completely dispelled from a field where approximately "one mosque was under way in every six hours", according to statistics declared by the authorities.[7] The mosques flourished especially in the unauthorised squatter districts on the fringes of large cities, where migrants from rural areas lived. As migration to towns confronted the dislocated population with an identity problem, the mosque functioned as a cultural anchor for the community. The form of the mosque, therefore, sustained its iconic nature by reproducing its stereotype image, often with false domes and minarets. Irony indeed reveals itself when the celebrated Ottoman mosques are compared to their contemporary versions in popular practice, with their odd shapes and proportions, mimicking their originals in tectonic crudity and pedestrian detailing.

One notable experiment in mosque design was marked by yet another battle over the mosque form (pl. 74). The idea of building a mosque within the parliamentary complex of a secular state gave rise to public controversy at the outset. For many, the integration of a mosque into the parliamentary campus was no less a betrayal of Republican principles than changing the secular principles stated in the Constitution. The response of the architects to this delicate matter has been to design an inconspicuous house of worship. Not only have the traditional elements been avoided, but the entire tradition of introverted and centralised space organisation has been cast aside. The prayer space extends alongside a full-length transparent *mihrab*, through which the space looks over a cascaded pool embedded in the slope. The transparency of the *qibla* wall is unprecedented in mosque architecture. The architects were not hesitant in exploring the past and present, nor the East and West, dispensing not only with stereotypes of the mosque but also with worn-out dualities and cultural polarities.

LIBERATION FROM THE MORAL CODES OF MODERNISM:
ECLECTIC COLLAGE AND NEW TEMPLES

Post-Modern relativism found its way into Turkish life with the Özal government (a parallel of Reagan and Thatcher in economy). In the first elections following the 1980 military coup, Prime Minister Özal represented a fusion of all tendencies into one: conservatism and progressivism, spiritual values and market values, the old and the new, East and West.[8] The architectural repercussions of this were stylistic plurality as a sign of cultural tolerance.

The new wave of the 1980s, continuing well into the 1990s, can be adequately described through the practice of a single architect: Merih Karaaslan (pl. 72). Themes he stressed in the justification of his work included pluralism, populism, symbolism and democratic tolerance. In his sketch for a project, the principles of an 'Anatolian Collage' are demonstrated as a mixture of Greek, Roman, Seljuk and Ottoman patterns. Official modernism in architectural competitions dissolved with his casual eclecticism and fantasy over cultural and natural forms.

Another field where eclecticism found thriving conditions was tourism developments, marked by the collage of another architect, Tuncay Çavdar. Themes taken up in his work included catchwords of Post-Modern culture: memory, allusion, quotation, irony, and metaphor. His architecture displayed a wealth of form and meaning, ranging from tectonic profusion to a medley of exotic images to set the scene for the average fantasy-seeking tourist. What was aspired to with the Hilton half a century ago was almost realised – mission completed for Turkey to become the new funfair of tourism. Hotel interiors staged all the signs of indulgence that orthodox Modernists could never stomach: paraphernalia and tacky decoration to be mistaken for temple interiors.

The concern with spirituality denied from the interiors of average mosques began to be lavishly provided for in hotels and shopping malls. With the proliferation of the atrium-type shopping mall, the growing consumerism built its new temples, with soaring bodies and volumes. The Post-Modern wave also uncovered the dormant reaction to secularism. During the 1990s, live TV programmes organised as an arena for public dispute staged Muslim activists as well as other critiques of the Republican principles. The Kocatepe Mosque complex turned into a hallmark of 'Post-Modern Turkey', as a perfect blend of faith and consumerism. The opening of a fashionable shopping mall right underneath the mosque was indicative of attempts to change the image of political Islam – tolerant and progressive in the use of modern technology and amenities. The mall was well adopted by secular circles and their opponents alike. Cultural plurality was tangible inside the mall: while cute girls in their micro garments performed their Christmas promotion tasks with Jingle Bell songs, veiled women wore their headgear in protest to the secular regime.

VERNACULAR HI-TECH AND HI-CLASS: THE SPREAD OF THE MEDIOCRE

Private sector investments became immensely varied from the 1990s. The revival of neighbourhood values in traditional communities and middle class settlements has been much stressed in popular TV serials. Their architectural counterparts in the market, however, are privileged enclaves for the upper class and the *nouveau riche*, marketed mostly with fake Ottoman imagery. While the aim professed is to recover urbanity and a sense of belonging, ironically, the result moves towards a loss of the public realm behind 'gated communities'. Guarded housing estates are designed in mixtures of eastern and western brands; besides types of Ottomania, advertisements of class privileges vary from 'California dream houses' to 'Babylonian terraces'. High-rise condominiums marketed under the rubric of 'intelligent building' are fairly new. While the claim for intelligence is confined to facilities such as the remote control of domestic tasks, ethical issues concerning the sustainability of resources are just not part of the question.

The expansion of the construction market over the past twenty years gave way to diversity and material wealth in the building sector, without much innovation in building technology. A new vernacular has emerged in the genre of antiseptic-hermetic buildings worldwide; displaying a deceptive high-tech imagery with their mirrored skins, these buildings share in fact a low technological profile confined to RC frames, wrapped up with façade systems, still in Botta or Hollein gestures. The profuse exploitation of imported materials, fixtures and finishes cannot conceal their cliché solutions. The most recurrent design approach in contemporary Turkish architecture presents a diversity based on such a 'play of forms', distinguished from each other by grand gestures materialised with variations on the bodywork. An architecture of 'mirrored bodywork' constitutes the new townscape of every settlement nowadays, from downtown Istanbul to its fringe developments and to all provinces where its influences reach.

The cumulative performance of architecture and city building in the past century seems to have fallen short of Modernist promises. Walking or driving through the streets of any town in Turkey gives one the poignant opportunity to contemplate the costs of brutal assaults on natural and historical assets, the devouring of urban lands by a greediness for rent, the erosion of the architectural heritage, and the spread of contractor- and ministry-styled vernacular modernism. Dissatisfaction with the anonymity of the emerging environment led architects to search for new routes. Prominent works aside, architectural production remained at a mediocre level, whichever direction has been followed: fake traditions and pseudo history as opposed to sheer pragmatism; assertive maniera and fabulism as substitutes for dry instrumental rationality. While the aim was to earn Turkish architecture an identity, an uncritical eclecticism emerged, whereby quality of design and craft was held secondary to image generation.

NEW DIRECTIONS IN REALISM AND AUTONOMY

The sudden liberation from the moral codes of Modernism and the exercise of excessive imagery and *laissez-faire* in architecture soon resulted in counter argument. Symposia and publications followed one another; occasions for professional debate increased, leading to an accumulation of architectural criticism and a building up of professional integrity. As distinguished products displayed in publications, exhibitions and award programmes helped to set standards, the repeated themes of Post-Modern eclecticism gradually became a bore. The National Exhibition and Awards programme of the Chamber of Architects was one of such occasions from 1988 onwards, where award-winning new designs and preservation projects became visible for comparison with the visual chaos and violence of mainstream practice.

Modern Turkish architecture can be said to have entered the new millennium with new directions in architecture. The products of a handful of architects, both senior and junior, point to a new realism that has emerged as a critical reaction to irrelevant formalism, pseudo history and fabulism. While the older generation presents examples that have distanced themselves from fleeting motifs, a younger generation, especially a group of Istanbul-based architects, has taken the lead in setting new standards and objectives (pl. 71). Their example is noteworthy in denying the 'external duties' undertaken by architecture — in other words, the representation of cultural identity or ideology.

The view that architectural form does not need pointing to a meaning other than itself, that architecture attains value primarily in a self-referential framework, is likely to introduce a new direction to the question of identity in architecture — towards the autonomy of architecture from the load of cultural dualities.

For illustrations of this article, the reader is referred to pls. 65-74.

[1] After being presented in the "Cultural Exchange Seminar" in Tehran (October 2002), a longer version of this paper appeared in an Iranian journal: "Architecture and Exercise of Identity: A Profile of Building Culture in Modern Turkey", in Abadi: Quarterly Journal of Architecture and Urbanism, (13: 38) spring 2003, pp. 20-45. The central theme expressed as 'cultural incertitude' concerning the question of identity is taken from an unpublished paper by the author: "Architecture and the Question of Identity: Buildings of Dwelling and Prayer in Post-Modern Turkey", presented at the Conference "Rethinking the Project of Modernity in Turkey", MIT Boston, March 10-13, 1994.
[2] Quotation from: Douglas Kellner, "Popular Culture and the Construction of Post-Modern Identities", in *Modernity and Identity*, S. Lash, J. Friedman eds., Blackwell, Oxford 1992, pp. 141-177 (142).
[3] Perfect accounts of the subject can be found in: Renata Holod, Ahmet Evin eds., *Modern Turkish Architecture*, University of Pennsylvania Press, 1984; Sibel Bozdoğan, Suha Özkan eds., *Sedad Hakkı Eldem, Architect in Turkey*, Concept Media, 1987. Observing this lightness and transparency achieved through generous openings in the timber Anatolian house, the historian Godfrey Goodwin is known to have once declared his wonder at why the Modern Movement had failed to emerge out of Turkey (anecdote by Professor Enis Kortan).
[4] According to anecdotes told on the occasion, Eldem was teased in the *Güzel Sanatlar Balo Gazetesi*, the 'Fine Arts Ball Gazette', with the following quip: "I have lost my identity in the Hilton; as I'll have a new one, the previous is invalid" (on the authority of Professor Feyyaz Erpi).
[5] Cited in Esra Akcan, "Amerikanlaşma ve Endişe: Istanbul Hilton Oteli", in *Arredamento Mimarlık*, 2001, 100+41, pp. 112-119.
[6] Two positions crystallised in a seminar held in 1984 by the Ministry of Culture to discuss the subject with professional and academic circles. See passages by Turgut Cansever and Doğan Kuban in: *Mimaride Türk Milli i-Üslubu Semineri*, Kültür ve Turizm Bakanlığı Yayını, Ankara 1984, pp. 23-30, 155-158.
[7] Head of Religious Affairs Mehmet Nuri Yılmaz declares a total of 69,523 mosques, 2,620 under construction, in *Yapı*, (168) November 1995.
[8] A critical account of the subject can be found in Sibel Bozdoğan, Reşat Kasaba, eds., *Rethinking Modernity and National Identity in Turkey*, University of Washington Press, 1997 (quotation: p. 147).

37.

Previous page
36. Suq al-Qattaneen, Old City, Jerusalem.

37. Al Madrasa al-Ashrafiyyah, Old City, Jerusalem.

38. The Dome of the Rock (7th century), Jerusalem.

39. Dar al-Aytam Complex, Old City, Jerusalem.

40. Al-Aqsa Mosque (8th century), Jerusalem.

41. The Old City, Jerusalem.

38.

39.

40.

41.

42-44. Association for Safeguarding
the Medina (ASM), reconstruction
of the Hafsia Quarter, Tunis, Tunisia, 1986.

43.

42.

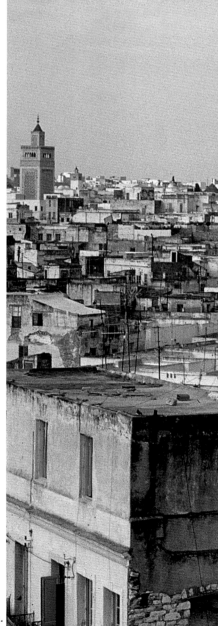

44.

45.

45, 46. Association for Safeguarding
the Medina (ASM), Oukalas Project,
Tunis, Tunisia, 1996-ongoing.

46.

47.

48.

47. Association for Safeguarding
the Medina (ASM), Al Montaciriya
Kindergarden rehabilitation,
Tunis, Tunisia, 1998.

48. Association for Safeguarding
the Medina (ASM), Douar El-Hicher
School extension, Tunis, Tunisia, 1998.

49.

49-57. Restoration Institute of Uzbekistan
and Restoration Office of the Municipality
of Bukhara, the restoration of Bukhara Old City,
completed in 1995.

49. Kalyan Mosque Complex (1127), Bukhara,
Uzbekistan.

50. Divan Begi Madrasa (1622), Bukhara,
Uzbekistan.

50.

51. Mir-i Arab Madrasa (1535/1556),
Bukhara, Uzbekistan.

52, 53. Abdul-Aziz Khan Madrasa (1651/1652),
Bukhara, Uzbekistan.

51.

52.

53.

54.

54, 55. Kalyan Mosque Complex (1127),
Bukhara, Uzbekistan.

56. Char-Minar Madrasa (1807),
Bukhara, Uzbekistan.

57. Mir-i Arab Madrasa (1535/1556),
Bukhara, Uzbekistan.

55.

56.

58.

59.

60.

61.

58. KEO International Consultants,
Nader Ardalan (principal designer),
Mercedes Benz Showroom, Kuwait, 1999.

59. KEO International Consultants,
Nader Ardalan (principal designer),
Khaldiya Apartments, Abu Dhabi, UAE, 2000.

60. KEO International Consultants,
Nader Ardalan (principal designer),
Al Ain Diwan, Al Ain, UAE,
anticipated completion 2006.

61. KEO International Consultants,
Nader Ardalan (principal designer),
Al Awadi Shopping Centre, Kuwait,
anticipated completion 2005.

62.

63.

64.

62. KEO International Consultants, Nader Ardalan
(principal designer), D'Agostino Izzo Quirk, Associated
Architects, Al Sharq Waterfront Marketplace, Kuwait, 1998.

63. KEO International Consultants, Nader Ardalan
(principal designer), Al Awadi Office Tower
and Shopping Centre, Kuwait, anticipated completion 2005.

64. KEO International Consultants, Nader Ardalan
(principal designer), Al Awadi Shopping Centre
Interior Atrium, Kuwait, anticipated completion 2005.

65.

66.

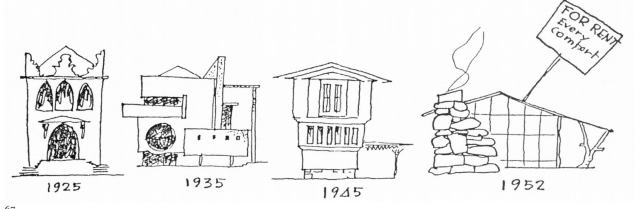

67.

68.

65. Arif Hikmet Koyunoğlu, Turkish Hearth Society, Ankara, Turkey, 1927.

66. Şevki Balmumcu, Exhibition House, Ankara, Turkey, 1933.

67. Caricature in *Güzel Sanatlar Balo Gazetesi* (Fine Arts Ball Gazette), 1952: "Architecture in Ankara".

68. Doğan Tekeli and Sami Sisa, Medicine Factory, Istanbul, Turkey, 1967.

69.

70.

71.

72.

69. Sedad Hakkı Eldem, Coffee House,
Istanbul, Turkey, 1967.

70. Sedad Hakkı Eldem and SOM, Hilton Hotel,
Istanbul, Turkey, 1952.

71. Murat Tabanlıoğlu, Turkish Pavilion,
Expo 2000, Hanover, Germany, 2000.

72. Merih Karaaslan, Peri Tower Hotel,
Nevşehir, Turkey, 1996.

73.

73. Turgut Cansever, Emine Ögün,
Mehmet Ögün and Feyza Cansever,
Demir Holiday Village, Bodrum,
Turkey, 1987.

74. Behruz and Can Çinici, Mosque
of the Grand National Assembly Mosque,
Ankara, Turkey, 1989.

74.

NEW PERSPECTIVES:
THE AGA KHAN TRUST FOR CULTURE

Urban Conservation in the Islamic World

STEFANO BIANCA

First of all, I would like to express my gratitude to our Iranian hosts for this opportunity to come to the old city of Yazd and to engage in a dialogue on urban conservation issues. Exchanging experiences in a field as complex as the rehabilitation of historic cities is always fascinating. While the specific conditions may vary from country to country, many common issues and problems emerge, these being the 'leitmotivs', as it were, of an endeavour to be shared by professionals, local communities, administrations and interested institutions.

Yesterday's site visit to the old quarters of Yazd confirmed my conviction that historic cities have in a way remained (or have become) villages in privileged locations; in other words, focal areas at the centre of rather anonymous, rapidly developing urban agglomerations. Today, these 'urban villages' are subject to all sorts of powerful pressures. Let me just mention some of the most obvious and ubiquitous factors:

- the impact of vehicular traffic and corresponding disruption of the physical and social fabric of the city;
- speculative real estate trends linked with vehicular accessibility which introduce new land-use hierarchies and disparities within the urban fabric;
- new standards of services, facilities and sanitation which usually are neither adapted nor integrated to the historic fabric;
- the demographic changes often involving the emigration of the wealthy local bourgeoisie from the historic centre to new residential suburbs, and, reciprocally, the immigration of a poorer rural population flocking into the cities and adopting the historic centre as a location of choice;
- crowding of a poor population in a partitioned historic housing stock with lack of maintenance;
- proliferation of uncontrolled semi-industrial activities in the historic city centre;
- and, perhaps most importantly, the loss of 'image' and prestige of the historic centres *vis-à-vis* the glamour of sometimes misconceived 'modernity'. This attitude results in a dramatic lack of investment by the private and the public sectors, denying the historic city the means it would need to evolve and transform from within, that is, following its own premises and potentials.

Yet, in spite of their relatively small size and all sorts of physical and social decline, it is these 'urban villages' which often remain the only custodians and dispensers of cultural identity in the metropolitan agglomerations mushrooming around them. Apparently a technology-driven development – regardless of the material progress it brought – has been unable to build upon (let alone replace) the cultural matrix from which historic cities have emerged and from which they drew their spiritual dimension, visual qualities and emotional comfort.

Facing this situation, we cannot avoid asking: why have historic cities – which used to be lively, creative and continuously evolving urban entities – suddenly become 'historic'? What is the rationale for a rather sterile type of conservation, which would freeze still-functioning buildings and urban districts like museal artefacts in an arbitrary stage of their evolution? Is there an alternative to rampant decline, eventual wholesale demolition and alien replacement?

My personal suspicion is that the museal conservation approach is nothing else than the shadow – or the logical response if you like – of a single-minded concept of modernisation and 'progress'. Both attitudes are interdependent and indeed united, inasmuch as they have equally lost sight of the wholeness of human existence and of culture as a primordial driving force of human life. This brings us right into the heart of the problem: the fatal dichotomy between 'conservation' and 'development', which acts like a dissolving agent in the complex, composite body of any living traditional culture, as soon as it becomes virulent.

Traditionally, culture always had a multi-dimensional quality because of its capacity to interweave material, emotional and spiritual concerns in successive loops of creative evolution. Its products thus had, by nature, the imprint of organic growth – similar to a beautiful garden, to take up Mr Beheshti's metaphor. Technological progress, in many cases, involves a reductionist approach based on abstract, rational procedures, isolated material concerns and exclusive economic considerations, which tend to ignore the richness of human potential and aspirations. If not inspired and balanced by other factors, technology-driven interventions can thus become highly destructive, particularly if they draw their energies and dynamics – as often happens – from disintegrating the complex web of local culture. No wonder that such abuses often result in the emergence of economically striving, but spiritually lifeless "urban deserts", to again quote Mr Beheshti.

Thus, through its very limitations and excesses, an aggressive type of narrow-minded, dogmatic development automatically calls for the antidote of an equally rigid conservation approach and the induced polarisation causes both sides to lose out. Excessive development – particularly if based on alien philosophies – finds it often impossible to set roots in the social ground and to acquire deeper meaning and truth, in other words, to engage people with their hearts and minds. Meanwhile, excessive conservation can suffocate and sterilise living cultural expressions, and can eventually become abortive to the creative impulses of a living community. Both extremes lead to a loss of real cultural presence: they deprive societies of the vital forces which could generate a self-reliant, 'organic' spiral of internal evolution.

Finding the productive middle ground between two sterile extremes is therefore essential for any cultural development effort, if it is to become fruitful. For one can neither afford to dispense with the creative sources of culture, nor disregard the material benefits of an appropriate 'domesticated' type of development. However, producing a creative interaction between culture and development is not just a matter of abstract strategies and procedures. It can only be achieved pragmatically, case by case, through emphatic immersion in concrete situations, through grounding actual projects in the realities of specific places and specific communities.

This means, on the one hand, promoting development by mobilising internal cultural processes, in other words, by designing projects which are rooted in the life of local beneficiaries and which can be sustained by them. On the other hand, it also means strengthening culture through adapted development impulses which rely on appropriate (and affordable) technological tools, provided they can be absorbed and managed by the actual stake-holders, the people directly concerned. To be successful, the rehabilitation of historic cities therefore has to go beyond mere restoration of monuments and other physical interventions. It must help re-activate and release the vital inner forces of local cultures and local communities. It must strengthen their capacity to creatively bridge the gap between past and future – in ways which are coherent with their own traditions and make the best possible use of their cultural and environmental assets.

**

After tracing the conceptual context within which the work of the Historic Cities Support Programme (HCSP) is taking place, let me now explain the operational parameters of the Programme within the Aga Khan Trust for Culture (AKTC) and the larger Aga Khan Development Network (AKDN).

While the AKTC deals with many promotional aspects of architecture, culture and the built environment in general – for instance through the Aga Khan Award for Architecture, ArchNet, the Aga Khan Programme for Islamic Architecture and the Central Asian Music Initiative – it is also actively involved in the restoration of historic buildings and conservation of historic cities. Accordingly, the HCSP was created to become the technical implementing agency of the Trust for all physical and social rehabilitation programmes in selected sites of the Islamic world, these projects being mostly funded by His Highness the Aga Khan. Funding and technical implementation being with the same organisation is a comparative advantage which has induced many other donors to provide co-funding to HCSP projects.

Through the AKTC, the HCSP is also part of the larger Aga Khan Development Network, which includes, among others, the Aga Khan Foundation and the Aga Khan Fund for Economic Development (AKFED). This means that it can rely on the interaction between culture and development by benefiting from the Foundation's track record in health, education and rural development projects, as well as from micro-credits and tourism investments provided by AKFED.

The HCSP's most prominent feature is the integrated character of its projects, combining interactively many different disciplines and concerns. While conservation and restoration of monuments and landmark buildings are central concerns, they are never done in isolation. The adaptive reuse of restored buildings – wherever possible – is considered from the beginning, in order to keep the building alive, provide meaning to the physical intervention, make local communities 'own' the building and generate income for future operation and maintenance. Planning the future development and improving the urban context of restored historic buildings is equally important. Problems of land use, vehicular access, sanitation and location of economic activities have to be considered, and all sorts of interventions from conservation to modern infill and sensitive redevelopment need to be defined and controlled. In connection with the urban context, rehabilitation of private housing in the historic centres is an essential issue, in order to keep the city alive, maintain an active social fabric and sustain the residents' commitment to their place of living and working. Direct funding of private housing improvement is often impossible and hence appropriate technical assistance, financial incentives and replicable pilot projects are required.

Another important theme of HCSP projects is upgrading and enhancement of public open spaces, an important element in historic cities, which connect monuments, houses and public facilities, and can provide a focus for social and cultural activities and strengthen the sense of civic identity and pride. Investments in public open spaces and parks can reverse the 'bad image' of complete districts and act as a catalyst for collateral private and public investment in historic areas.

Apart from physical improvement projects, the HCSP in most project locations pursues associated socio-economic development activities and local capacity-building. Such projects may include revival and promotion of local skills and crafts (sometimes as an offspring of restoration activities), vocational training, small enterprise support, placement of unemployment labour, micro-credits, projects in the fields of health, women and youth affairs, promotion of cultural tourism and corresponding events. In many cases, they are linked to the reuse of restored or rehabilitated buildings located within the domain of the communities concerned. This can also give rise to the formation of new local associations and NGOs which become actively involved in the sustainable operation and management of their heritage and their built environment.

Training and institution-building are also major concerns in the constitution of the Aga Khan Cultural Service Companies – local affiliates of the AKTC and the HCSP in important project locations which are entrusted with the implementation and management of project activities under the supervision of the headquarter staff from HCSP Geneva. They are also assisted by a roster of international experts in various technical fields whose prime task is to train capable local professionals and motivate them to carry on.

***

So far, the Historic Cities Support Programme is or has been pursuing revitalisation projects in seven quite different regions of the Islamic world: in the Northern Areas of Pakistan, Zanzibar, Samarkand, Cairo, Mostar (Bosnia-Herzegovina), Syria and Afghanistan, including over twenty distinct projects, some of them interconnected and mutually reinforcing. In general, HCSP interventions are planned very pragmatically, and while they start from an overall vision, they do not proceed according to abstract, preconceived schemes. Rather, they are based on gradual incremental growth in response to actual needs, perceived opportunities and feed-back from field experience. Involvement in single project locations or regions tends to expand in order to constitute a critical mass for positive change, if the environment is found to be responsive. In all project locations, community participation, training of local professionals and local institution-building are essential components. While overall agreements with central government authorities are usually sought for HCSP projects, the actual work proceeds in as close cooperation as possible with local government and stakeholders. Many other institutions, such as the Getty Grant Programme, the World Monuments Fund, the Ford Foundation, the Swiss, Swedish and Norwegian bilateral aid organisations and the World Bank have provided co-funding or collateral funding to HCSP activities.

In the Northern Areas of Pakistan, HCSP activities are focused on the high valleys of Hunza and Baltistan, in the Karakorum range. This whole area, a part of the old Central Asian Silk Route, was inaccessible to vehicular traffic until the construction of the Karakorum Highway in 1978. Increased accessibility, coupled with the impact of tourism, has induced a rapid transformation of local societies and economic patterns, which calls for strategic development visions and procedures capable of steering ongoing rapid change.

Projects in Hunza and Baltistan include the restoration of several old forts and palaces (such as Baltit and Shigar) and other landmark buildings in conjunction with the rehabilitation of traditional settlements, as well as promotion of traditional crafts and construction techniques (pl. 80). Villages and neighbourhoods which were in danger of being deserted in favour of dispersed modern construction in the fields are now being rehabilitated through the active efforts of residents – a fact which not only boosts cultural awareness efforts, but also helps preserve the precious terraced landscape and reduces costs for infrastructure provision. Preserving local identity and at the same time introducing contemporary living standards (including sanitation) has been the key to the ongoing cultural development process, which is undertaken with the active involvement of the local population. Environmental planning strategies to preserve specific cultural assets in the light of growing tourism are now being implemented through new local institutions such as Town Management Societies and Cultural Heritage Trusts.

In Zanzibar, the focus is on the Old Stone Town, one of the few truly cosmopolitan cultural sites in Eastern Africa (pls. 85, 86). It had its key days in the nineteenth century, when it became a meeting point between Omani, Indian (and, later, European) influences merging in the Swahili culture. Political upheavals in the 1960s resulted in major demographic and socio-economic changes. Many of the beautiful old houses from the Omani period have been partitioned and are in lack of proper maintenance.

Within the Old Stone Town, the HCSP has completed the restoration of the former Old Dispensary, the Old Customs House and the conversion of the former Extelcom building – formerly empty landmark buildings on the waterfront now being put to new uses, some of them related to tourism. In parallel, a conservation plan for the Old Stone Town has been prepared in cooperation with the Stone Town Conservation and Development Authority. A number of community-based housing improvement projects are being carried out to demonstrate the feasibility of traditional low-cost repair and maintenance techniques – a key issue for the survival of the Old Stone Town. A new urban design plan and an economic strategy are currently being prepared for the rehabilitation of the complete historic waterfront as a significant civic open space which, once enhanced, would spark further rehabilitation efforts in the Old Stone Town.

The old city of Cairo is arguably the most important historic city in the Islamic world. While it has lost much of its pre-industrial urban fabric, its wealth of important monuments from various successive dynasties is unrivalled. The pressures emanating from the eighteen-million-persons metropolis on the historic city centre are enormous (particularly in terms of roads and vehicular access) and remaining green areas have become extremely scarce.

The HCSP's involvement in Cairo started with the conversion of a vast barren site (a hilly rubble-dump between the Fatimid city and the Mamluk cemetery) into a thirty-hectare urban park with many visitors' facilities (pls. 75-77). This landscaping project will not only bring relief to the dense metropolitan agglomeration, but will also help transform the image of the adjacent old city and mobilise resources for its rehabilitation. As part of the grading effort on the park slopes, 1.5 kilometres of the formerly buried twelfth-century city wall were brought to light and are now being restored. Near the wall and inside the district of al-Darb al-Ahmar, several mosques, old palaces and historic houses are being rehabilitated in an effort to revitalise the existing architectural heritage and make it accessible to the local community as well as visitors. In conjunction with physical upgrading, a wide range of socio-economic initiatives have been launched to provide residents with new opportunities, including training, employment, micro-credits for small enterprises, health centres and women's associations. Many restored buildings are being reused for community purposes, in order to enhance the identification and solidarity of residents with historic buildings. Owners and tenants are also being provided with technical assistance, small grants and loans for housing improvement.

In Samarkand, another landmark city of Islamic architecture, the monuments have suffered from the stripping of their historic urban context and from their discontinued use (or conversion into museums) during the Russian period (pl. 83). Even the colonial and the modern city centre are in need of more convivial spaces.

In an effort to close these gaps through appropriate infill projects, the HSCP has assisted the municipality in preparing a new master plan for the Timurid city, including urban design proposals for the revitalisation of both the historic and the modern city centre. In addition, a number of pilot projects have been carried out in cooperation with local residents to demonstrate how the historic neighbourhoods can be upgraded without need for wholesale demolition and excessive redevelopment.

The war-struck city of Mostar is a rare example of a partly Muslim city in Europe, with a long tradition of inter-cultural exchange and cooperation which came to an abrupt end with the collapse of former Yugoslavia (pls. 81, 82).

Projects here concentrate on the rehabilitation of the historic neighbourhoods adjacent to the famous Old Bridge (which is being restored by the joint efforts of UNESCO and the World Bank) and on the restoration of a number of key monuments destroyed during the civil war. Within the framework of a complete master plan for the old city, several historic buildings and open spaces have been restored in close cooperation with the local authorities and residents, reclaiming the unique character of this multicultural city.

The Islamic heritage of Syria is rich and complex, as it is often built upon (or reuses) pre-Islamic structures of Roman-Hellenistic, Byzantine or Crusader origins. Due to historic circumstances and topographic opportunities, Syria features a large number of citadels, some of them isolated, some of them now in the heart of historic urban agglomerations.

The Syrian Directorate of Antiquities requested the HCSP to provide technical assistance and training for the conservation of three major citadels in Aleppo, Masyaf (pl. 84) and Qalat Salah ed-Din. The ongoing conservation work on the monuments is now being complemented by the establishment of detailed site management plans, as well as by environmental studies aimed at controlling and enhancing development in the surroundings of the three forts, two of them being located within an urban context, and one in a pristine natural setting.

In Afghanistan, an age-old cultural heritage has been under threat due to decades of political un-rest, religious and ethnic conflicts, and interventions of foreign powers. In terms of Islamic culture, Afghanistan occupies a pivotal position, being an offshoot of Persian culture and a spring-board for the Mughal accomplishments in India.

After the end of the civil war, an agreement was concluded by the AKTC with the Interim Admin-istration to restore, rehabilitate and upgrade a number of important historic buildings and public open spaces in Kabul. These include the Park of Babur (the oldest Mughal 'paradise garden') and the Timur Shah Mausoleum, an important landmark set in the midst of the old markets and adja-cent to a former garden and the Kabul riverbanks (pl. 79). Rehabilitation efforts have also been ini-tiated in the historic residential neighbourhood of Ashkan i-Arefan in cooperation with local resi-dents. Similar efforts are being considered for the heart of the old city of Herat, around the Chahar Suq area.

Having presented the current portfolio of the Programme, it should be said that the HCSP has no ambition to systematically cover complete regions, let alone the whole of the Islamic world. Rather it proceeds by selecting a limited number of project locations in the expectation that they will en-able the Programme to demonstrate how a small-scale but integrated project set-up can be brought to fruition by a number of interactive initiatives rooted in the respective local community – or, in other words, how mutually supporting efforts in various domains, focussed on a clearly identifiable site and group of people, can coalesce into a critical mass and spark a self-propelling cultural de-velopment. While the initial investment often has an experimental character and involves heavy training components by external experts, everything is done to make later phases of the project as replicable as possible, maximising the use of local expertise and reducing project costs. Later phas-es of work also tend to show higher enrolment of local resources, as the demonstration effect has con-vinced people of the feasibility and can stir productive competition between local communities.

For illustrations of restoration projects by the Aga Khan Historic Cities Support Programme (HCSP), the reader is referred to pls. 75-86.

Our Works Point to Us: Restoration and the Award

RENATA HOLOD

It is a real pleasure to return to the hospitable walls of Yazd where many years ago I began to study the secrets, wonders and curiosities of Iran's architectural heritage. My study had been aided not only by local officials and families but also by the prevailing attitude of respect for, and use of, the built environment, and by the live memories invested in these walls. These in turn were supported by the ongoing tradition of local histories, beginning with the sixteenth- and seventeenth-century ones such as the *Ta'rikh-i Yazd* and the *Ta'rikh-i Jadid-i Yazd*, and the *Jami'-i Mufidi* to Iraj Afshar's *Yadigarha-ye Yazd* of the 1970's.[1]

Today, Yazd looks very different. The urban sprawl reaches far into the historic hinterland of formerly far-off gardens and Zoroastrian memorial complexes, and the historic city proper within its walls and with its fifteenth-century extensions seems small, overwhelmed and half-empty. On the other hand, areas that were far beyond the pedestrian extent of the old town, such as the major gardens, are today the main recreation areas and lungs of the conurbation. Thus, it is most appropriate to have Yazd be the place for a seminar that takes stock of the uses of the past, and the future of buildings and environments so carefully remembered and celebrated by past writers and users.

A reassessment for all uses and strategies connected with conservation and restoration is critical. It comes at a time when the present-day urban sprawl has dwarfed the area of the historic zone to a fraction of the built-up area. The result has distanced the inhabitants of every city from the historic fabric in actual and emotional investment. Historic centres have emptied of the families and social networks that had ensured continuity, rebuilding and repair to be replaced by new populations and over-densification in the best of circumstances, or to be left to complete abandon and ruin.

Inna atharna tadalla 'alaina; fa 'anzuru ba'adna illa al-athari
"Thus our works point to us; gaze after us at our works"

These are words from Arabic wisdom literature but also pertain very much to the topic of my talk today. The saying crops up commonly in a variety of popular literature and circumstances.[2] It has also been recorded as being used in this very region of Yazd and its province. The historian Mohammad Mufid Mostawfi Bafghi mentions it in his interesting and important digest of historical works, the *Jami'-i Mufidi*, written in 1671-1679 (later half of the eleventh century AH). This is the very text of the inscriptions, which Khanish Begum, a sister of Shah Tahmasb and the wife of Nu'aym ad-in Ni'amatullah Baqi ordered written for remembrance of her and her deeds. The words were repeated in four corner galleries (*ghorafah*).[3] Built unusually large to hold her with her attendants, these form the second storey in the mosque that was appended to the *khanaqah* of the Sufi Sheikh Shah Ni'amatullah Vali Kirmani. In pursuing her programme of enlargement and radical change of the *khanaqah*, Khanish Begum (and her master builders) would not have worried much about the propriety of altering the physical fabric of the previous building nor about retaining all of its aspects. In fact, so encrusted is this complex with additions and accretions that it is difficult to make out all aspects of even this addition. These challenging words of Khanish Begum are nowhere to be seen presently under the many layers of whitewash. Yet all this change happened in the flow of time when the systems of knowledge and meaning were continuous and continuously refreshed from the same sources.

Today, the luxury of adding and changing built environments at will without self-consciousness of time past and present simply does not and cannot exist. Our approach to this monument and similar complexes comes at a moment when there is no longer an assumed continuity of building practice; in fact, rupture and discontinuity of practice must be taken as real. Those who work in and with historic environments must grab at the tattered strings of local building knowledge and learn its orders. To impose today's needs and to utilise today's tools directly on the remnants of the delicate historical fabric is to help, if not speed up, the process of its disappearance. Single monument or urban matrix, the development and application of restoration, conservation and reuse programmes are fraught with difficulties and frustration.

It is, therefore, with a full realisation that heroic efforts were necessary to carry out even the smallest restoration and conservation project that the Aga Khan Award for Architecture created a place in its system of recognition and awards for projects of restoration, conservation and reuse. Thus, in another sense, the individual awarded projects and the sum of the recognised projects also point to the Award. The road travelled towards their recognition, and the development of its own criteria for excellence in these sectors of the built environment of the Islamic world have formed the history of thinking about the historical built environment within the Award itself. Beginning with the first Awards in 1980, the key approaches to historic structures and environments were recognised: restoration, restoration and adaptive reuse, reconstruction and conservation strategies.

What follows is a review of the awarded projects with a summary of their achievements. In passing, aspects of the projects, which deserve further notice, which reveal some shortcomings, or which have remained unanswered must be mentioned as well. Initially, we at the Award were so pleased to find any successful project that, perhaps, achievements were highlighted and spotlit, and shortcomings shaded or diminished. But, in the stretch of twenty-five years and eight Award cycles, the scope of the projects (both considered and awarded) has expanded, while criteria for evaluating them have been sharpened and refined. In sum, the strict criteria for recognising restoration projects were kept, while the category of the reuse of historic fabric was expanded to include projects that could be best described as reconstruction and conservation initiatives, with attention to programming reuse in the historic fabric, with community engagement and support as well as institutional involvement.

As always, the pursuit of restoration remains a highly skilled and technical process. Only three restoration projects have been awarded: monuments in Isfahan, Multan, and Jerusalem. Archaeological study (and publication), the careful use of reversible processes, a clear definition of the old and new fabrics, the multiplier effect of on-the-job training for craftsmen and technicians were clearly programmed into the long-term efforts to save these major monuments.

In the case of Isfahan, the generative effect of the restoration has extended well beyond the monuments themselves (pls. 1-3, 89, 90). They have been published in an exemplary manner, and the record of their construction process has contributed immeasurably to our knowledge of the practices of building of the Safavid period and of early modern Iran in general.[4] The process of restoration of the individual pavilions with their structural complexities and complex decorative programmes has generated a group of artisanal professional specialists whose skills have been applied to other, similar buildings. The restoration project has reached into the entire complex of the Maidan-i Shah, and from it into the historic urban fabric of Isfahan.

The result has been the safeguarding of the Safavid centre. Much after the recognition of the restorations in 1980 by the Award, one of the recommendations of the original programme was implemented, namely the pedestrianisation of the *maidan*, and the removal of the inappropriate garden layout in its centre. The blocking of traffic circulation from the *maidan* has meant that the structural well-being of the Safavid monuments has been safeguarded. The reintroduction of the open ground on the *maidan* brings it closer to its original urban concept of a large multi-purpose space where a variety of temporary events and structures could be staged. The historic city area has been expanded further to include more of the original territory of the Safavid palace zone. By moving government offices to other venues, additional pavilions have become available for public uses like, for example, the Museum of Natural History, or Gallery for Contemporary Art. Such an expansion has provided a historic park/conservation zone within the heart of a rapidly expanding and densifying metropolis that now stretches several miles beyond the furthest reaches of the great Safavid gardens of the Hezar Jarib and that also includes newer industrial suburbs and developments. The creation of a historic park has meant that the function of the great bazaar must be rethought as it no longer continues to operate as the main commercial centre of this conurbation. This historic area, nevertheless, should be seen in contradistinction to the virtual erasure of much of the medieval city fabric in Isfahan through the continued insertion of large avenues through it, and the rapid destruction of the housing stock within it. The restoration of the Safavid palaces and the safeguarding of their physical context, then, is a signal example. It deserves worldwide continuous study and recognition for its large scale as well as detailed successes.

Shrines, whether urban, suburban or rural, have marked the landscape of all the regions of the Islamic world. Many have become derelict when their popularity diminished or when they lost incomes from their *waqfs*. Many have survived and flourished to this very day, supported by endowments and individual gifts. Their continued existence in the twentieth and twenty-first centuries is evidence of their hold on popular piety and imagination. The Shrine of Rukn-i-'Alam, the Suhrawardiya saint of the eighth/fourteenth century, standing in Multan, Pakistan, fell on bad times when the income from its endowments diminished and when its maintenance was no longer carried out (pls. 92, 93). The restoration campaign of 1971-1977 differed from the previous repairs in important ways.[5] In addition to stabilising the platform on top of which the mausoleum sits, special care was taken to drain the site properly and to replace rotting timbers. New industrial materials were used very sparingly. Significantly, the campaign revived or recreated fourteen different building and decorating crafts, among them the tile mosaicists. The practioners of these crafts have gone on to work on other historic monuments controlled by the Awqaf, or into the private sector. The restoration was funded through a special fundraising campaign initiated by the conservation branch of the Awqaf Administration, and carried out through the governorate of Punjab. A major monument has been restored and returned to use.

There is no question that the Haram al-Sharif and its great monuments are the focus of continuous attention in Muslim piety and imagination. The Masjid al-Aqsa, as important as the Dome of the Rock, has undergone many more structural changes and repairs, the last of which in the 1950s and 1960s created adverse conditions for the monument itself through the introduction of concrete and anodized aluminium in the dome. The disaster of an explosion and fire in 1969 threatened the integrity of the dome and destroyed much of the painted decoration. An expert restoration was initiated by the Al-Aqsa and Dome of the Rock Restoration Committee with the support of the International Centre for the Study of the Preservation and Restoration of Cultural Property (ICCROM).[6] The campaign succeeded in restoring the damaged parts of the building to the highest restoration standards, being careful to distinguish any new infill work from the original (pls. 40, 91). The process of the project also produced two crucial generative effects. First, it resulted in the training of restoration workers. Secondly and significantly, the restoration committee expanded its purview to include all areas of the Haram al-Sharif, with work continuing in subsidiary areas and plans to engage in similar high quality restorations there. It is still hoped that a full account of the restoration work on the Masjid al-Aqsa as well as on the Shrine of Rukn-i-'Alam will be presented in print.

Finally, these two latter awarded projects are important demonstrations of the fact that major religious shrines and centres can be repaired and rebuilt with careful attention to their historic features. The urge to repair need not result in covering everything with new materials and green paint.

Such is the press of the new, and such are the casualties of the present day that often the pure restoration process with its stringent requirements is not enough or is not possible. In those cases, other intermediate strategies could yield positive results.

The conflicts in Lebanon of the late 1970s and 1980s resulted in many victims, including much of the built environment. A notable example was the Great Omari Mosque at Sidon, shelled and bombed by the Israeli forces (pls. 87, 88). The will and the resources to rebuild its shattered fabric came specifically from Rafiq al-Hariri. The building had been in a poor state of repair and had undergone many previous repairs, many of those in the 1950s-1970s ultimately damaging its historic fabric due to the use of inappropriate materials, but the 1982 destruction rendered it unusable. This reconstruction, undertaken under the conditions of military occupation, was understood to be as much resistance to this occupation as it was repair of the severely damaged building.[7]

The fate of many residences of past elites has been an unhappy one, and few have escaped intact. One such example has been the Azem Palace in Damascus. Originally built in the mid-eighteenth century for Assad al-Azem, one of the last great Ottoman governors of the province, it was arranged around three courts. Its representative function was recognised by the French as well, and during resistance to the French occupying forces in the 1920s it was severely damaged.

Wholesale or partial reconstruction for emotional reasons must be recognised, while it cannot be deemed restoration because little of the original fabric survives. Memory of place and function is then paramount in returning meaning or even reinventing it for an important location.

All regions within the Islamic world are left with old capitals and their palaces; should these remain as museums alone? Or should their very existence, given their considerable open grounds and generous public spaces, be harnessed for present uses for the ever increasing populations that surround them: recreational park space, educational programmes, training courses or simply lungs for the city?

The generative effect of individual efforts to recuperate something of the historical fabric were recognised: whether it is the anchoring of a view of a bay for a vacation house, or the much more involved and ambitious energising of an entire small community around the creation of an Art Festival, the result can radiate beyond the individual project.

From the onset, large scale conservation efforts were brought to the attention of the Award process. Through these projects, it is clear that the validation and valuation of the historic built environment is a very difficult, complex and never ending process requiring constant attention and watchfulness.

The following must be asked when considering strategies for the conservation of the urban fabric:
- local ordinances: long-term?
- development short-term gain, long-term loss?
- cooperation among participating agencies?
- restoration and/or adaptive reuse?
- urban fabric and/or monuments?
- living entity or museum town?
- government programmes and/or private sector investment?
- rediscovering the old house?

All these and more strategies and tactics must be constantly in use. The most successful projects are never perfect, while even partially realised ones have something to contribute to our kit of tools.

For illustrations of Award-winning projects of restoration, the reader is referred to pls. 1-3, 40 and 87-93.

[1] The results of this study are partially available in my dissertation and in entries on Yazd in Lisa Golombek and Donald Wilber, *The Timurid Architecture of Iran and Turan*, Princeton 1988.

[2] For example, it is also found in the preface to the album of Bahram Mirza, composed by Dust Muhammad, see the translation by Wheeler Thackston, *Album Prefaces and Other Documents on the History of Calligraphers and Painters*, vol X, Muqarnas Supplements, Leiden 2001, p. 11. The saying has also been attributed to Imam Ja'afar Sadiq and/or Jabir ibn al-Hayyan, see Syed Nomanul Haq, *Names, Natures and Things*, pp. 5-6, 15.

[3] The habit of writing on walls of interiors may also be a reference to the Hermetic tradition of inscriptions in caves, as reported through Jabir ibn al-Hayyan, see Nomanul Haq, *Names* cit., p. 206.

[4] For a detailed description of the restoration project see the 1980 Awards in Renata Holod and Darl Rastorfer, *Architecture and Community: Building in the Islamic World Today*, Aperture, New York 1983, pp. 184-197. The Isfahan project was undertaken by the combined forces of the National Organ-isation for the Conservation of Historic Monuments of Iran (NOCHMI) and the Italian Institute for the Middle and Far East (ISMEO) beginning in 1964. Occupancy for Ali Qapu was 1975, for Chehel Sutun and Hasht Behesht, 1975-1980. The following publications present the first results of the restoration: Eugenio Galdieri and Roberto Orazi, *Progetto di sistemazione del Maydan-i Shah di Isfahan*, Rome 1969; Eugenio Galdieri, *Apparenze e realtà nell'architettura Safavide*, Venice 1978; Giuseppe Zander (ed.), *Travaux de restauration des monuments historiques en Iran*, Rome 1969. Subsequent impact studies have yet to be done.

[5] For details of the restoration work see the publication of the 1983 Awards, Sherban Cantacuzino (ed.), *Architecture in Continuity: Building in the Islamic World Today*, Aperture, New York 1985, pp. 173-177.

[6] Awarded in 1986. For details see Ismail Serageldin, *Space for Freedom*, Butterworth, London 1989, pp. 118-131.

[7] Awarded in 1989. For details see James Steele, *Architecture for Islamic Societies Today*, Academy Editions, London 1994, pp. 39-45.

Appreciating High Technology

SUHA ÖZKAN

The present session is dedicated in particular to the appreciation of technology, preferably 'high technology', since we are aware of the interest of Iranian architects in this subject. We are all aware that the most sophisticated architecture and its subsequent discourse is created where construction forces its limits as far as contemporary building technology allows. The Aga Khan Award for Architecture aims to validate appropriate architecture for Muslim communities, therefore my presentation will be limited to those projects that have a particular emphasis on the creative use of technology.

Throughout the history of the Aga Khan Award for Architecture, its juries have placed an emphasis on 'appropriate technology', that is to say the technology related to the materials and methods of construction that are appropriate to the potentials of various geographical locations, especially in places where building materials are scarce. The juries have given awards to projects that experiment with building materials and that deal with new construction techniques using material abundant in the vicinity.

Sometimes emphasis was placed on compact bricks or large building blocks made out of desert sand, as was the case of the Agricultural Training Centre, Nianing, Senegal. Sometimes the Award was given for making more intelligent use of the abundantly existing volcanic stones on site, like the Stone Building System, Daraa, Syria. There are many projects that aim to develop local technologies for building, and all these would be considered in line with the teachings of Hassan Fathy.

When we examine the Awards from the point of view of advanced technology, in almost every cycle we find projects that have addressed the creative use of contemporary building technology. In the first cycle of the Award (1980), the Master Jury gave an award to the Hotel and Conference Centre in Mecca, Saudi Arabia. In this conference centre and the hotel next to it (with 170 rooms), but especially in the conference centre itself, the German architect Frei Otto used tensile structures inspired by popular and prevalent traditional tent designs.

Metal cladding was applied to these tensile structures. The interiors have been illuminated with modernised traditional light fittings, while other decorative elements were applied in order to be conversant with the ambiance of this Holy City. The tensile structure had steel pipes or columns which transferred the load to the exterior. The whole structure was stretched by these outer columns, and cables stabilised and connected them to the ground. In the central polygonal courtyard, lighter sun-breaking decorative elements formed a kind of latticework. The courtyard was covered as an extension of the tensile structure of the main building and it was embellished with natural landscaping elements in order to soften the hard metallic presence of the design.

The aluminium cladding was designed in such a way that it would emulate or have some association with the desert tents of the region. The rest of the building, the hotel and the mosque were constructed in a reinforced concrete structure with traditional desert stone cladding. The texture of the outer walls refers to the traditional mosques and the colours and building materials of the region. The mosque and the minaret are strongly associated with an existing historical mosque with its corner minaret, and steep stairs up the side. This detail in the project has become a symbolic reference to the traditional mosque in a modernised version. There was some association with the widespread contemporary technology of reinforced concrete structures with stone cladding and tensile structures, used creatively in reference to traditional building modes.

In the Tuwaiq Palace, Riyadh, we can witness a more or less similar approach (pl. 94). Here the building itself is one undulating wall, which defines an interior space. This wall creates a barrier between the harsh desert climate of Riyadh and what has been contained within the large lush green courtyard.

The author of this project is Omrania whose chief architect is Basem Shihabi. It is similar to the previous building in that the tensile structures were also designed by Frei Otto, who is perhaps *the* master of this type of design in the twentieth century. The curvilinear wall is eight hundred metres long. It accommodates all the facilities that the building houses: guest rooms, conference halls, meeting places, restaurants, leisure areas; in short, everything a building like a diplomatic club needs to have in a capital city where the diplomatic community is very important. All entertainment and sports areas, which require large gatherings, are accommodated in the tensile structures projecting out of the continuous wall into the desert landscape and sports fields.

These tensile structures are made of woven reinforced plastic fabric, bound by polyester resin with surfaces treated with dust repellent Teflon® coating. The generic idea of this building is to confine a protected space in a desert climate where the outside environment is harsh but obviously dramatic to see. The contained space inside is treated like an oasis.

The wider outside environment has been planned and planted according to a very sophisticated landscape concept that is based on regenerating extinct species which resisted during the long period of desertification. The Riyadh Diplomatic Area Landscaping project, another Award-winning design, regenerated these species using a meticulous process of sifting desert sand into fine dust and keeping it in incubators, thus giving life to plants that were no longer known to exist. The saplings have been replanted as landscaping elements which do not need irrigation to survive and grow. This is the result of a meticulous process of research and development.

After many years of being exposed to sun and dust the tents have not collected any dust, since this has been repelled by the Teflon® coating and drifted away with the wind. The canopies function admirably well. In the places where this building opens to the internal lush, green, well-maintained and irrigated courtyard, the high-technology tensile canopy covers the semi-open space in the courtyard as well.

The joining lines and details of the natural stone cladding and the steel structure are honestly expressed wherever they occur. The points where they interact with the main building surfaces are articulated in the form of well-designed details as a gesture of celebration of technology where stone cladding and steel structural elements meet.

These details in many places produce their own composite order or perhaps some kind of abstract artistic expression which again can be regarded as a celebratory gesture *vis-à-vis* high technology. Inside the courtyard, on both the courtyard and terraced outside walls, a rich landscaping was executed. The building was also intended to incorporate soft elements of landscaping together with hard stonework and a fine finish of steel and reinforced plastic canopies.

The third building of interest is a dramatic one. It is a huge 'high-tech' canopy offering protected space to shelter three million pilgrims every year. The Hajj Terminal, Jeddah, Saudi Arabia, was built for pilgrims coming to Mecca (pls. 98, 100). The main purpose of the terminal is to accommodate the transferral of pilgrims from the aircraft to buses that take them to the Holy City of Mecca. The Terminal is used only one month each year but in a very intense way. It was designed by Skidmore, Owings and Merrill, where the chief designer was Fazlur Rahman Khan, a Bangladeshi engineer, who also conceived the whole structure of the famous Sears Towers in Chicago.

This is a vast complex where each module measures about fifty-two metres with two and four post-column structures holding the structure firmly at the edges. In the main area, where corners of each group of four canopies meet, there are large round steel columns. Each module is covered by a single-surface, reinforced plastic tent. The site plan is very simple, with two structures placed on each side of a highway. It emanates a very serene and horizontal presence as a light tent structure punctuating the desert shape of Jeddah. The structure is permanent but at the same time it has the quality of lightness that would be associated with periodical or temporary use.

The tensile bars hold the structure together and carry the top. The reinforced plastic membrane is stretched at the top level of the masts or columns and they are reinforced by cross wiring. The columns were connected at the top and in the middle by deep steel beams to prevent buckling and to resist lateral forces. A series of lateral members form square boxes on the edges. This is the first vast use of reinforced plastic and steel and woven plastic fabric material on such a large scale. It has lasted over twenty years, again with minimal maintenance, or none whatsoever.

The prospective pilgrims to Mecca land here first. The Hajj Terminal is the welcoming point for their passport clearance and emigration formalities and here they are distributed into small groups and guided by their local counterparts (*daleels*), the believers' hosts who will guide them through pilgrimage to the proceedings in Holy Mecca.

The basic idea of this structure is to provide shelter and comfort from the dust and sun and nothing more. Under this shelter there is an enormous activity of welcoming the prospective pilgrims or saying 'goodbye' to the accomplished *Hadjis*. During the preceding and succeeding weeks of *Eid ul Adha* about three million people are dealt with here under this vast space. Provisions are rudimentary and simple, but very clean: fresh water, refreshments, toilets and telephones – naturally facilities for eating and relaxing have been laid on. All this has been provided for by making use of the highest possible technology and there is also very good lighting in this space. The strong rays of the sun are filtered through the membrane during the day and reflected floodlights brighten the space at night. All the facilities that any airport should have are temporarily located here; souvenirs or shopping areas mark the historical presence of this unique life time experience.

This building has been given a special kind of architectural Award particularly for its ingenious structural solution and the space it defines for a unique Muslim activity that occurs once a year. The Master Jury of the Aga Khan Award for Architecture (1983) considered this accomplishment as 'appropriate technology' as regards to its unique and specific purpose in accommodating an important ritual of Islam. It also has its own drama as a very elegant structure.

It may be debatable whether the Water Towers of Kuwait are high-technology structures or not, but the construction technique of casting on the ground and raising the top pieces was applied here for the first time in Kuwait (pls. 97, 99). This is a project again designed by western consultants, the Swedes Sune and Joe Lindström, who provided a very powerful expression for these water towers. At the time when these towers were built (1976) water was even scarcer, and having water accumulated and stored at higher elevations was convenient for distribution and easier than using pumping stations. The architects referred to two aspects of Kuwaiti culture. One looked to the history of the Kuwaiti population, who have been pearl divers and merchants over the centuries: the pearl trade is still an important activity in Kuwait. The other source of inspiration came from palm trees and oases. In this project both are referred to in very abstract and elegant forms. The architects avoided simplistic analogies and did not fall into the trap of banality while emulating natural forms. These are not copies of palm trees, but abstractions of palm trees.

The architects arranged these structures in the form of batteries of twelve or sixteen grouped towers. This assembly makes a distinct reference to oases, home always to water, and the groupings also provide shelter from the sun and landscaped areas. They quickly became landmarks like some kind of man-made oasis and in order to distinguish and give identities to each one of these oases they were treated differently. The construction system consisted in erecting stems and then sliding formworks upward. The top tanks were cast at ground level and then lifted up. Finally the binding concrete was poured up in small quantities. This technology was used here for the first time on this scale and this magnitude in Kuwait.

Another Award-winning project which is worth citing here is the Arab World Institute, located in Paris, France, designed by Architecture-Studio (whose lead partner Rodo Tisnado is participating in this conference) and Jean Nouvel.

The idea generating construction of the Arab World Institute in Paris was conceived by French industrialists and exporters, who were encouraged by the late President François Mitterand, as an appreciative gesture towards Arab countries – an act of embracing their culture in Paris (pls. 162, 163). Architects Jean Nouvel and Architecture-Studio (Rodo Tisnado) were very sensitive to the townscape of Paris and made this very special contextual building an integral part of Paris University. The site is in the vicinity of Notre Dame Cathedral on the embankment of the River Seine.

In using the most sophisticated building technology possible, the architects imagined a façade, which has been conceived like latticework. Lattice is a common craft form in almost all cultures, Islam being no exception. The façade is a huge screen, a lattice or maybe a *mashrabiyya* of Arab building tradition. The approach from the city is through a narrow and well-defined square gate court where the visitor sees the building in fragments; he then enters the main square which is a vast plaza defined only by one side screened by the lattice of the façade.

The architects developed an ingenious method of light control in this lattice in the form of contracting and expanding diaphragms. Many different types of apertures of the façade let the sun's rays into the internal spaces in proportion to the intensity of the sun and a predetermined comfort level of luminosity inside. They work like the apertures of cameras. It is a wonderful experience inside; when the sun goes behind the clouds there is much activity on the façade which adapts itself to the increasing or decreasing level of sunshine to be allowed in.

When this project was technically reviewed for the Award, the Award office engaged a parallel review by a Parisian architect-anthropologist to measure the reaction of Arabs in Paris in order to find out how they regarded this very unconventional building. To our surprise, almost seventy percent of them said they were very happy to have a high-technology progressive building to house and represent their culture. But this is simple to understand: Arabs in France are contributing to the creation of Ariane rockets, Airbuses, Peugeots and Citroens; their aspiration is for their own original culture to be represented by the highest level of technology. They must be tired of their culture being represented by carpets, socks, clothing, their folklore and nothing else, and so they embraced this building as part of Arab culture in Paris. It is a building full of surprises. There is always a major exhibition of one or two aspects of Muslim culture going on in the Institute. And again, sunset becomes a defining experience when it is viewed from within the structure.

The last building I am going to present is another project which celebrates high technology; the small tower designed by the architect Ken Yeang, who is also participating in this conference. I will simply attempt to explain why it won an Aga Khan Award.

For some time, all tall buildings were seen as being contradictory to the idea of environmental friendliness or the passive use of cooling systems and air circulation. With the IBM headquarters in Kuala Lumpur, Malaysia (pl. 95), architect Ken Yeang has proven that one can create tall structures and skyscrapers that use environmental forces for the benefit of comfort in a building. In his diagrams, the movement of air in the building is sketched in a way that shows that natural forces can also provide air circulation and passive cooling efficiently (pl. 96).

While incorporating natural forces Ken Yeang does not compromise his own liberty of architectural expressiveness; he uses technology and the forms of his free interpretation, but bases them functionally on his philosophy of environmentally-friendly building systems. As Charles Jencks has said, this type of work belongs to a school of thinking in contemporary architecture which makes use of ecological forces and endeavours to interact with them in an environmentally-friendly way.

Small landscaped courtyards with vegetation on the periphery also add to the cooling, while at the same time providing a more pleasant relationship between the inside and the outside of the building. The interface between 'in and out' is not a simple rigid glass pane but a stretch of nature which multiplies positive effects.

This is what we have accomplished with the Aga Khan Award for Architecture in terms of the appreciation of 'high technology'. As you know we have given Awards to more than ninety projects; it is not possible to present all of them in such a limited period of time.

For illustrations of Award-winning projects concerned with high technology, the reader is referred to pls. 94-100, 162 and 163.

Celebrating Islamic Tradition: Looking Ahead

PETER DAVEY

The Aga Khan Awards for Architecture have become a cultural institution of great importance, not only to Muslims but to the whole world. They were started in 1977 and are selected every three years by distinguished international juries. They are intended, as the first prospectus said, to "awaken the cultural consciousness of Muslims, and to sensitise those who would build in the Muslim world to the unique heritage of Muslim art and architecture". The aim remains to "nurture within the architectural profession and related disciplines a heightened awareness of the roots and essence of Muslim culture, and a deeper commitment to finding meaningful expressions of the spirit of Islam within modern life and technology." "Consideration will be given," said the founding statement, "particularly to those projects which use local initiatives and resources creatively, which meet both the functional and cultural needs of their users and have the potential to stimulate related developments elsewhere in the Muslim world."

Over the years, the Awards have maintained these principles and so have taught us all a very great deal. By embracing the whole of Islamic culture, the Awards have opened the eyes of the world to the extraordinary diversity of the Muslim achievement. They have made those of us from the West (and, I think, many Muslims) aware that the Islamic inheritance ranges from Central Africa in the south to Central Asia in the north, from Morocco in the west to Indonesia in the east. By celebrating conservation of buildings from the past as well as new work, the Award scheme has made us all recognise the wonderfully rich interwoven tapestry of the climates of the Muslim world: climates which are cultural as well as physical, conceptual as well as contextual. The architectures celebrated are largely urban in the widest sense, because it is in cities, which the Award has rightly interpreted to range from small settlements to large and ancient centres of habitation, that civilisation rises. (Indeed, the very word 'civilisation' in English is derived from *civis*, the Latin word for a person who lives in cities. There must be similar constructions in other languages and cultures.) Incidentally, this celebration of the diversity of Muslim civilisation has made us aware of the extremely deep roots of Islamic architecture, which draws on the best aspects of pre-Muslim cultures to generate appropriate buildings, towns and cities.

As a westerner, I was of course aware of the influence of Byzantine architecture on that of the Islamic Eastern Mediterranean, but the ways in which, for instance, the traditional buildings of the

Subcontinent and of South East Asia had informed Muslim work were unknown to me. One of the perennial fascinations and excitements of the history of Muslim architecture is how ancient work was modified and enriched by the arrival of the new religion, so we get quite different architectures and urban textures throughout the Islamic world, though naturally they are all informed by the same ethos. Of course, such continuity and diversity in architecture was generated by an implicit understanding of climatic, material, physical and economic imperatives.

The diversity of work recognised by the Awards is multiplied by their explicit understanding of the economic imperative, and the Award scheme deserves great praise for accepting that architecture is for all: rich and poor alike. I was very puzzled when I saw that, in the first cycle of Awards, *kampung* improvements in South East Asia were celebrated at the same time as modern buildings like large hotels and posh villas, along with restorations of fine ancient monuments and beautiful old towns. I was wrong to be so. Improvement of life for the poor must be at least as vital in any decent society as catering for the needs of the more affluent. By sometimes (indeed often) focussing on work for some of the very poorest people in the world, the Award scheme has shown that architectural intelligence can radically affect the lives of everyone, in ways that were completely unimagined by even the most ambitious social engineers of the early Modern Movement in the 1920s and 1930s. And the scheme has shown the world that such intelligence and vision is not limited to those of us who have undergone the very long formal architectural educational system. One of the great virtues of the Awards is that they are set up to recognise excellence in creating the human-made world, no matter what the source.

Through the Award scheme, I have met African masons and Asian carpenters who have had at least as much influence on their fellow citizens as the most elaborately western-trained architect or planner. On the other hand, I have also been introduced by the Award to architects and planners who have done amazing work by building on tradition. I do not mean by this kitsch-copying of traditional forms, but by deeper understanding of why such forms were there in the first place, immemorially honed by need and understanding of material necessity and human aspiration. And how such understanding can help knowledge of our ancestors' achievements serves us all today in using new technologies and systems of thinking. In this connection, the Awards' recognition of the importance of conservation is very important.

Celebration and encouragement of conservation of fine old buildings and city quarters serves several very important ends. First, old buildings remind us of the achievements of our ancestors. Whether they were made for princes or peasants, what we inherit was built by our predecessors and, in a sense, it belongs to all of us. A culture without historic buildings is almost as poverty stricken as a culture without literature or science. Second, old buildings provide us with lessons: each generation has different things to learn from its ancestors, so it is vital that we not only learn in our own time, but carefully pass on the buildings to our successors, so they can find their own lessons. Third, having real old buildings in our midst shows the absurdity of kitsch-copying (which is sadly becoming common all over the world). By comparison with the real thing, a new building that uses old forms, transferring masonry and timber to concrete and plastic, decoratively and without thought seems simply absurd. Just as historical dialogue between past, present and future is culturally vital, so is geographical communication between the peoples living on the planet today. Instead of accepting the assumption (common in both the Muslim world and the West) that the poor must learn only from the rich and try to ape what has happened in developed (often over-developed) countries, the Award scheme has set up dialogues between affluent and disadvantaged. It is becoming clear that, living in a world with limited resources, we all have much to learn from each other. The architecture (and indeed the economy and culture) of the affluent has much to gain from lessons that seem natural in much of the poorer parts of the world: for instance by maximising ambient energy of radiant heat from the sun, the cooling power of the oceans, the ground and the winds; lessons about economical use of space, by understanding how to use local resources to most efficient effect. In short, by learning about how to try to live in creative harmony with the planet.

Ismail Serageldin has written most movingly about the Muslim concept of "stewardship of the earth". Exercise of this stewardship, he says, involves two complementary strands. First, "the pursuit of 'development of the earth', 'taming' nature to serve man's purposes, cultivating its resources and increasing its bounty. This pursuit is that of a steward, not a rapacious exploiter." Second, says Serageldin, "the society of men who work this earth and enjoy its fruits and bounty must be organised in a just and mutually supportive manner: [in] a 'justly balanced' society". Serageldin wisely remarks that "I do not believe that the reading of the Koran at any level will provide detailed instructions on how to design a house in Morocco or Indonesia, or how to design the thoroughfares of Cairo or Istanbul. If God had desired to give people specific instructions on how to build structures in the twentieth century, He could certainly have done so explicitly." Rather, study of the sacred texts should produce appropriate responses to problems confronting Islamic societies today and tomorrow. Such thinking should inspire us all, Muslims and others alike.

Globally, we are faced with various varieties of ghastly built fungus which surround every city on the planet from Sana'a to Samarkand, Tokyo to Tunis, Damascus to Detroit. Countryside is consumed by these corrosive environmental diseases at an increasing and unsustainable rate, while these plagues progressively erode the cities that gave them life in the first place. In the developing world, such explosive growth is largely caused by the poor flocking to cities to try to make a better living. In the West, the effect is reversed (particularly in North America), with the middle class fleeing to the suburbs from cities, which, as a result, become increasingly derelict. Such changes in the structure of cities are immensely important: they threaten civilisation and the planet itself. I am not in the least trying to argue that in Muslim and other developing countries, there should not be population movements from countryside to suburban areas. For the foreseeable future, such migrations are inevitable. Humankind, it seems, is irrevocably bound to be an urban species, and learning how to deal with the exploding cities of the world is without doubt the most important physical and social problem facing us today. We need creative responses. The Awards have shown how effects of the migrations, normally so humanly and environmentally destructive, can be greatly mitigated by sensible and thoughtful initiatives. Such schemes not only reduce the often horrifying results of mass urban immigration but, by involving the dynamics of the people who are moving, they set positive models for development of all kinds. Many (but not all) such initiatives recognised by the Awards have been put in train not only by architects and planners, but by people as different as bankers and bureaucrats, engineers and educators, religious leaders and social reformers. In fact, whatever the source of initiative, it is almost always local communities that have been the sustaining force in such developments. The Award scheme is unique in recognising the importance of how developments are regarded by their users. No other architectural awards even try to look at such issues. Other awards are largely concerned with appearance: with flashy pictures and presentation, not existential reality: not with what it is really like to live and work in the projects. The Aga Khan Awards explore such matters by sending assessors to examine the buildings after at least one year of use. Such careful assessments ensure that permeated projects are potentially sustainable, and have won the approval of their inhabitants. Suha Özkan has called the process the seeds of "democratisation of the environment", and I think he is right. If only other prizes had the resolution and resources to pursue such an approach, rather than chasing cheap headlines, we might begin to make a huge change in the quality of architecture and planning, and their potential for improving the lot of humanity.

Aga Khan Award-winning work offers robust examples that others can learn from, and the magnificent archive of the Awards is a testimony to what has been achieved and a reference source for all who want to study contemporary Islamic architecture, conservation and the structures of the developing world. One of the most important aspects of the Awards is their long-term vision. Buildings take such a long time to create, and their effects on people are so hard to assess, that only long-term investment in thorough research can ensure that an award system is likely to improve the practice of architecture and planning. So, even after a quarter of a century, it is still too early to judge what the results of the Aga Khan Awards will be. Subjectively, I feel that there has been a gradual movement towards many of the ideals that the Awards have been in the vanguard of promoting: sustainability, understanding of tradition and history, democracy (or participation), taming global homogenisation, and promoting regionalism. When the Awards were born, these issues were scarcely on the spectrum of architectural consciousness. But now, as Suha Özkan has said: "The well-being of mankind and care for the environment have become our top priorities, in great contrast to the immediate past's focus on economic development which, left unchecked, caused damage that may prove irremediable." He is right, but progress has often been slow, and there have been some discouraging setbacks. For instance, twenty years ago, regionalism was thought to be perhaps the most important way of combating the endless spread of international cultural schlock, making architecture more responsive to local physical conditions and creating buildings and cities that could help us interpret our particular cultural inheritance to our children, positioning us as the hinge in the cultural continuum between past and future. But the horrendous Balkan and Central African wars of the 1990s made many of us think again about regionalism. What had seemed to be ideals which would enrich and provide human focus in the ever expanding anomie and human indifference of the international post-modern capitalist system seemed suddenly to be soaked in blood. What had been hoped for as a means of establishing individual and communal identity could become a justification for violence and intolerance. What had been supposed to be a proposal for living in harmony with the planet seemed to be unleashing untamed destruction. Yet it is time to reconsider the notion of regionalism. We do need a sense of placedness in the world, not least to counter the proliferation of environmentally destructive mediocrity. We need to evolve architectures that are appropriate to locality, and to stop the absurd and catastrophically wasteful practice of creating identical buildings from the Equator to the Arctic. We need to understand and master the wonderful but potentially destructive powers of modern global technology and communications, and how to adapt them appropriately to particular circumstances. Because the Aga Khan Awards have continued to promote their founding values of celebrating 'local initiatives and resources', they have shown how new and richer ideals of regionalism and urbanism can be attempted. They have consistently celebrated courage, imagination, tenderness and nobility in the creation of the human-made environment of the Islamic world. So they have shown how architecture can better human life and enrich our relationship to the planet. Long may they continue to inspire all of us.

For projects that have won the Aga Khan Award for Architecture, the reader is referred to pls. 1-9, 12, 16, 40, 42-44, 49-57, 73, 74, 87-95, 97-109, 162 and 163.

76.

75-86. Restoration projects by the Aga Khan
Historic Cities Support Programme (HCSP)
in various locations.

Previous page
75. HCSP, aerial view of the site for Azhar Park
under construction, Cairo, Egypt, 2000.

78.

76. HCSP, main spine, Azhar Park, Cairo,
Egypt, 2004.

77. HCSP, the Ayyubid city wall (12th century)
bordering Azhar Park, Cairo, Egypt,
restored in 2003-ongoing.

78. HCSP, Khayrbek Complex (16th century)
located between the Darb al-Ahmar spine
and Azhar Park, Cairo, Egypt, restored in 2003-2005.

79.

80.

81.

82.

79. HCSP, Timur Shah (19th century), Kabul,
Afghanistan, restored in 2003/2004.

80. HCSP, Baltit Fort, Karimabad,
Pakistan, restored in 1992-1997.

81. HCSP, Lakcica House, Mostar,
Bosnia-Herzegovina, restored in 2002.

82. HCSP, Muslibegovic House, Mostar,
Bosnia-Herzegovina, restored in 2000-2002.

83. HCSP, housing upgrading with the dome
of the Gur-i-Emir, Timur's funerary mosque
and tomb, in the background, Samarkand,
Uzbekistan, 1998.

83.

84.

85.

84. HCSP, Castle of Masyaf (12th century), Masyaf, Syria, restored in 2002-2004.

85. HCSP, Zanzibar Old Stone Town, Zanzibar, Tanzania.

86. HCSP, The Old Dispensary (19th century), Zanzibar, Tanzania, restored in 1994-1997.

86.

87.

87, 88. Saleh Lamei-Mostafa, Great Omari
Mosque (late 13th century), Sidon, Lebanon,
restored in 1986.

89, 90. Italian Institute for the Middle
and Far East (ISMEO; Eugenio Galdieri)
and the National Organisation
for the Conservation of Historic Monuments
of Iran (NOCHMI; Bagher Shirazi), Ali Qapu
(1660), Isfahan, Iran, restored in 1977.

91. Isam Awwad and the International Centre
for the Study of the Preservation and
Restoration of Cultural Property (ICCROM),
Al-Aqsa Mosque (14th-century paintwork),
Jerusalem, restored in 1983.

88.

89.

90.

91.

92.

92, 93. Awqaf Department, Tomb of Shah
Rukn-i-'Alam (14th century), Multan,
Pakistan, restored in 1977.

93.

94.

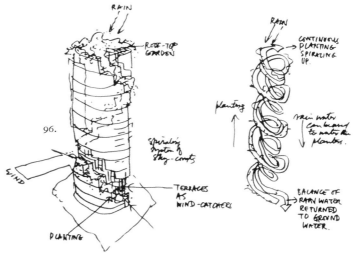

96.

94. Atelier Frei Otto, Buro Happold,
Omrania, Tuwaiq Palace, Riyadh,
Saudi Arabia, 1985.

95. Hamzah and Yeang, Menara Mesiniaga,
Selangor Darul Ehsan, Malaysia, 1992.

96. Drawing by Ken Yeang.

95.

98.

99.

100.

97. VBB and Björn and Björn Design,
Water Towers, Kuwait, 1976.

98. Skidmore, Owings and Merrill,
Hajj Terminal, Jeddah, Saudi Arabia, 1981.

99. VBB and Björn and Björn Design,
Water Towers, Kuwait, 1976.

100. Skidmore, Owings and Merrill,
Hajj Terminal, Jeddah, Saudi Arabia, 1981.

101.

101, 102. Grameen Bank Housing Project,
various rural areas, Bangladesh, 1984-ongoing.

102.

103.

103, 104. Zlatko Ugljen, Sherefuddin's White Mosque,
Visoko, Bosnia-Herzegovina, 1980.

104.

106.

107.

105. Falké Barmou, Yamaa Mosque, Illela-Yaama, Niger, 1982.

106, 107. ADAUA/Fabrizio Carola, Kaedi Hospital, Kaedi, Mauritania, 1989.

105.

108.

108, 109. Patrick Dujarric,
Alliance Franco-Sénégalaise, Kaolack,
Senegal, 1994.

109.

ANSWERS FOR THE FUTURE

The New Paradigm in Architecture

CHARLES JENCKS

A change of heart, a new vision for architecture? If there really is a new paradigm in architecture then it will reflect changes in science, religion and politics and it does not take a clairvoyant to see that George Bush & Junta (as Gore Vidal calls them) are very much locked into a medieval world view (if that isn't an insult to the Gothic). No, the reigning disciplines are struggling with primitive orientations and will continue to be so until one catastrophe or another (global, ecological?) forces them to shift gears, there is no widespread cultural movement underway. Nevertheless, one can discern the beginnings of a shift in architecture that relates to a deep transformation going on in the sciences and in time, I believe, this will permeate all other areas of life. The new sciences of complexity – fractals, non-linear dynamics, the new cosmology, self-organising systems – have brought about a change in perspective. We have moved from a mechanistic view of the universe to one that is self-organising at all levels, from the atom to the galaxy. Illuminated by the computer, this new world view is paralleled by changes now occurring in architecture.

Several key buildings show its promise – those by Americans Frank Gehry, Peter Eisenman, and Daniel Libeskind. There is also a vast amount of other work on the edge of the new paradigm by the Dutch architects Rem Koolhaas, Ben van Berkel and MvRdV, or the Europeans Santiago Calatrava and Coop Himmelblau, or those who have moved on from high-tech in England, such as Norman Foster. These architects, as well as those that flirted with Deconstruction – Hadid, Moss, and Morphosis – look set to take on the philosophy. In Australia, ARM (Ashton Raggatt MacDougall) has been mining the territory for many years and another group, LAB, has completed a seminal work of the new movement, Melbourne's Federation Square. Soon there will be enough buildings to see if all this is more than a fashion, or change of style, but it certainly is the latter.

The emergent grammar is constantly provoking. It varies from ungainly blobs to elegant waveforms, from jagged fractals to impersonal datascapes. It challenges the old languages of classicism and modernism with the idea that a new urban order is possible, one closer to the ever-varying patterns of nature. One may not like it at first, and be critical of its shortcomings, but on second glance it may turn out to be more interesting, more in tune with perception than the incessant repetition of colonnades and curtain walls.

The plurality of styles is a keynote. This reflects the underlying concern for the increasing pluralism of global cities. Growing out of the Post-Modern complexity of the 1960s and 1970s, Jane Jacobs and Robert Venturi, is the complexity theory of the 1980s, which forms the unifying idea. Pluralism leads to conflict, the inclusion of opposite tastes and composite goals, a melting and boiling pot. Modernist purity and reduction could not handle this reality very well. But the goals of the new paradigm are wider than the science and politics that support it, or the computer that allows it to be conceived and built economically. This is the shift in world view that sees nature and culture as growing out of the narrative of the universe, a story that has only recently been sketched by the new cosmology in the last thirty years. In a global culture of conflict this narrative provides a possible direction and iconography that transcend national and sectarian interests.

To see what is at stake one might start with those at the edge of the new tradition and see how they differ from those closer to the centre. I would call them Organi-Tech architects because they reflect both their Modernist parents, the high-tech architects who used to dominate Britain, and their grandparents, organic architects such as Frank Lloyd Wright and Hugo Haring who tried to parallel natural forms. Organi-Tech, like its twin 'Eco-Tech', straddles both sides of this duality; that is, it continues an obsession with technology and structural expression while, at the same time, becoming more ecological. The contradictions and hypocrisies this leads to, are openly admitted by Ken Yeang, who acknowledges that while the skyscraper is very un-ecological by nature it is hardly going to disappear as the corporate type of choice. So, like Foster, Piano and other Modernists committed to this reality, he aims to make them less environmentally costly. Richard Rogers is committed to this policy at the regional scale and currently making heroic attempts to change the entropic urban trends of Britain. Other Organi-Tech designers produce surprising structural metaphors that celebrate the organic nature of structure, the bones, muscles and rippling skin of an athlete at full stretch. Both Nicholas Grimshaw and Santiago Calatrava have designed expressive skeletons meant to dazzle the eye, especially when the sun is out (pl. 111).[1] They are filigreed light-traps, or pulsating exoskeletons that show our bodily relation to other organisms. One cannot help being moved by these spectacular constructions even if their message often may be too obvious.

Yet, while relating to nature and exploiting the computer in design these architects have not accepted the rest of the new philosophy. This is evident in several ways, particularly in their handling of structure. This they make, in the manner of Mies van der Rohe, excessively repetitive. They conceive prefabricated elements that are identical, or in mathematical jargon "self-same rather than self-similar", boringly replicated rather than fractal. Most of nature – galaxies, developing embryos, heartbeats and brain waves – grows and changes with minor variations. This insight was finally given a scientific basis by the late 1970s, after the computer scientist Benoit Mandelbrot wrote his polemical treatise *The Fractal Geometry of Nature* in 1977. It took more than a decade before the idea was assimilated by architects, and translated into computer production for building. But by the 1990s it led to the promise of a new urban order that, like a rainforest, is always self-similar and always evolving slowly, an order more sensuous and surprising than the duplication of self-same elements. Perception delights in fractals, in a slightly varying stimulus, which is why, at dinner, it is better to compare wines than stick with the same one. Endless repetition dulls the palate, as Organi-Tech designers show when they multiply a good idea to exhaustion. Think of Renzo Piano's beautiful Kansai airport, the same interesting airfoil shape extruded for a whole mile, until it is boredom squared. Architects, by contrast, who use fractals – Libeskind, ARM, Morphosis – literally give us a break from their standard forms, and the young group LAB and Bates Smart have already pushed beyond these first experiments and refined the grammar.

Another identifiable group, producing *rounded* fractals, were recently christened "Blobmeisters" in New York. The label implies several truths, not all of them flattering. First that these 'meisters' were determined to capture the field, and do so with 'blob grammars' and abstruse theories based on computer analogies – cyberspace, hybrid space, digital hypersurface were some of the other terms. Often the "Blobmeisters" were young university professors and their students engaged in the usual turf wars. Greg Lynn, easily the most creative and intelligent of this group, has argued in a series of books that the blob is really a developed form of the cube. It can handle more information than the dumb box; its complexity and therefore sensitivity are potentially greater. But this is not the case, if the grammar is not scaled and phrased with skill and correlated with function. So many blobs are simply the result of stacked geodesics, like Grimshaw's Eden project, a series of bubble-forms that remind me of what geologists call globular clusters – enticing, edible, squashy in appearance. But these creations can sometimes be awkward, for instance around the entrance, or where they meet the ground or another structure. Norman Foster's two giant blobs, one for the Mayor of London the other for a new music centre in Newcastle, have these problems. The internal space and structure are more convincing than the way they relate to the city. By contrast, his Swiss Re Headquarters building is a perfected, stretched blob conceived as a city landmark. It started off life as an egg shape and then, after wind and structural studies, re-emerged as other natural metaphors – not only the far-fetched gherkin of the tabloids, but a more plausible and welcoming pinecone and pineapple. The spiral skycourts and aesthetic refinements give further rationale to these metaphors, making them multivalent and enigmatic in a plausible way, as I will argue. Once again the computer helped produce self-similar forms at an acceptable price. The entasis of this skyscraper, like that of a Doric column, leads to a new kind of propositional beauty, one worked out digitally (pl. 115).[2]

Foster's partial shift from a Cartesian to blob grammar marks a turn of mainstream practice towards the new paradigm. It follows many sculptural experiments, for instance those of Will Alsop in Marseilles and Frank Gehry in Europe, Japan and America. Ever since Gehry's New

Guggenheim opened in Bilbao, in 1997, architects realised a new kind of building type had emerged, and that there was a standard to surpass. His landmark building (telling euphemism for what used to be called a monument) pulls this former industrial city and its environs together – the river, the trains, cars, bridges and mountains – and it reflects the shifting moods of nature, the slightest change in sunlight or rain. Most importantly its forms are suggestive and enigmatic in ways that relate both to the natural context and the central role of the museum in a global culture. Indeed, because of what is called the Bilbao Effect, the enigmatic signifier has become *the* reigning method of designing large civic buildings, especially museums. This emergent strategy, which started in a small way during the 1950s with Ronchamp and the Sydney Opera House, has now become a dominant convention of the new paradigm. Peter Eisenman, Rem Koolhaas, Daniel Libeskind, Coop Himmelblau, Zaha Hadid, Morphosis, Eric Moss – and now mainstream architects such as Renzo Piano – produce suggestive and unusual shapes as a matter of course, as if architecture had become a branch of surrealist sculpture. It has, and the results may often be overblown, pseudo-art, but it is worth examining the multiple causes of this shift.

The chief negative reasons are cultural. With the continual decline of the Christian and Modern belief systems, with the rise of consumer society and a celebrity system, architects are caught in a vicious trap. They have little, if any, credible public conventions and ideologies to build for, they lack any iconography beyond a debased machine aesthetic (or High Tech) and an ecological imperative that has yet to produce accepted symbols, so they are pushed and pulled in opposite ways. The absence of all beliefs leads them to a degree zero minimalism, a good expression of neutrality, but of course one that is totally absorbed into the reigning system. By contrast, a competitive culture demands difference, significance, and fantastic expression in excess of the building task. The enigmatic signifier responds to this conundrum. The injunction is: you must design an extraordinary landmark, but it must not look like anything seen before and refer to no known religion, ideology or set of conventions. In the 1910s the artist Giorgio de Chirico, faced with similar perplexities, was asked what he painted and replied, "the enigma".

The enigmatic signifier in the hands of Gehry can work well because he labours over the sculptural aspects of the form and light and adopts multiple metaphors that relate, albeit loosely, to the building's role. Thus in his Disney Concert Hall, the overtones of music and cultural brio were interpreted with clashing petal forms, ship metaphors and symphonic images. At Bilbao many critics found similar allusions to fishes, ducks, trains, clouds and the adjacent hills (pls. 112, 113).[3] One excited writer acclaimed the structure a "Constructivist artichoke" – see analysis – another a "mermaid in metallic sequins". Several of these organic overtones might be appropriate to the central place of art in the city today, the museum as cathedral; some might be subjective or accidental. But, with the best work in the new paradigm, these metaphors are more than random projections, the outcome of a Rorschach test or automatic, unconscious creation. They are emergent, multivalent signifiers in search of an open interpretation, one related to the building task, the site and the language of the particular architecture. The idea of the 'open work' of art has been in the air since Umberto Eco proposed it as a typical response of artists and writers in the 1960s. Now, for social reasons, it has emerged more fully into architectural view. As the monument has mutated into the landmark building, as architects have lost most conventional iconography, they now hope to find through a process of search and invention, some emergent metaphors, those that amaze and delight but are not specific to any ideology.

Again this search is aided by computer — all Gehry's curved buildings are produced this way, and at only little more expense than if they had been constructed from repetitive boxes. While he candidly admits he does not even know how to switch on a computer, and uses the machine to perfect and manufacture forms worked out sculpturally, younger architects exploit the generative aspects of the digital revolution. Dutch architects, in particular the group MvRdV, construct datascapes based on different assumptions and then allow the computer to model various results around each one. These are then turned into designs and presented polemically to the press, the public and politicians. Alternative societies are contrasted in their "Metacity/Datatown" of 1998 (pl. 132); for instance Holland as a high consumption Los Angeles is opposed to a country of thrifty vegetarians. The built implications of these choices are then exaggerated and turned into an ironic, democratic poetry. It is democratic because the data are a result of collective laws, building codes, straw poles and debated choice; it is ironic because these various forces conflict and often contradict each other, producing bizarre results; and it is poetic because the consequences are presented in deadpan, colourful juxtaposition. One case in point is their sheltered housing for the elderly, another their Dutch Pavilion for Expo 2000 (pl. 116).[4]

This last humorous construction alternates floors of open greenery and enclosed workspace, then surmounts them with wind turbines and a roof garden. At the top a pond collects rainwater and it is circulated throughout, forming an efficient cycle along with the heat re-circulated from the auditorium below. Ecological motivations alternate with economic efficiencies, nature's cycles intermingle with human activities. One floor is a grid of trees in pots whose bases penetrate the floor below forming an interesting sculptural ceiling. Strange and sometimes appropriate associations are made. Edible plants and flowers occupy floors in repetitive rows, recalling the factory farms of Holland, which mass-produce a remorselessly standardised nature. An exterior stairway wraps the open and closed volume like a coil of black DNA. Semi-transparent screens and varying colours classify the activities like boxes of data on the computer screen. In effect, the forces at work in the Dutch system are handled digitally and emerge in unlikely new combinations. At this point a sceptic will ask how all this differs from the old Modernist commitment to treating the city as a mere summation of statistical forces, the very thing Jane Jacobs and the complexity paradigm criticise. Well, it has to be admitted that much of the thinking here, as elsewhere, is a carryover from the past.

The neutrality, the acceptance of urban and commercial forces as given, the pragmatism and opportunism are hardly a step forward. To reiterate, the new paradigm is at the beginning, not the middle or apex of its development and many architects such as Calatrava and MvRdV are only partially engaged with it. But, at the same time, these and other Dutch architects, and so many of the young exploiting cyberspace, also use the data as creative tools. Their datascapes are often truly emergent structures, as well as Dadascapes, new forms of bottom-up organisation not possible to realise before the advent of fast computation.

The same is true of another identifiable trend of the new paradigm, the emergence of the landform as a building type and its correlate, the waveform organised around a new grammar of strange attractors. Peter Eisenman has led the way with his Aronoff Centre in Cincinnati, a staccato landform that oscillates around a strange attractor of chevrons and zigzags. It looks in part like the jiggling of tectonic plates, an earthquake, the basic metaphor of the earth as a constantly shifting ground rather than the terra firma we assume. Matter comes alive in this architecture on a gigantic scale. His City of Culture in Santiago de Compostela, now under construction, is another undulating landform that picks up the surrounding landscape as well as other generating metaphors, the local emblem of the Coquille St Jacques and the adjacent medieval city.

Coop Himmelblau, like Morphosis and Zaha Hadid, has won several recent competitions with a wave-like landform – the schemes for a museum in Lyons, and a BMW centre in Germany. Then there is the LAB landform already mentioned, the one built by Enric Miralles in Alicante and those of Ben van Berkel under way. These ten or so artificial grounds really do constitute an emergent urban type, but the one that really put it on the architectural map was FOA's Yokohama Port Terminal, designed in 1995 and finished just before the final of the 2002 Soccer World Cup (pl. 114).[5] Part urban infrastructure and part civic space for sunbathing, festivals and public events, it has the mixture of activities typical of other landforms. Again it was conceived inside the belly of a computer, and the architects Moussavi and Zaero-Polo are quite proud about the way they were surprised by the emergent results, even when they did not like them ("an alienating artistic technique" to which they are, ironically, un-alienated). Shades of Park Hill Sheffield and automatic writing? They eschew the obvious wave and maritime metaphors, but there is no reason for the public to follow suit. This is just one more, exciting, enigmatic signifier.

I believe it is the job of architects to take responsibility for the public and esoteric meanings of a civic building, whether enigmatic or not, but this is an especially difficult task in a global culture without a shared value system. The temptation is to hide behind social and technical requirements, to use supposed determinants to suppress symbolism. Perhaps the only architect of the new paradigm who admits to both larger spiritual concerns and a public symbolism is Daniel Libeskind. His Imperial War Museum-North, outside Manchester, explicitly symbolises the various kinds of war (on land, sea and in the air) as well as a globe that is fragmented by strife (pl. 117).[6] He constantly invokes the cultural and emotional plane of expression as the duty of the architect; he is not afraid of facing up to the fundamental issues of meaning and nihilism that silence other designers.

Libeskind won the competition for Ground Zero in New York because he faced the symbolic and spiritual issues of the problem both specifically and with the more allusive enigmatic signifier. Rather than be an inadvertent metaphor of death (the "skeletons and hanging bodies" of Vinoly's solution) or an evasive techno-abstraction (as were some of the other entries), he was specific about certain memorial signs: for instance, the "wedge of light" and the "1776 Tower" (both an ascending spiral and sign of the Statue of Liberty). At the same time the slashes, spirals of crystals and abstract slurry walls were suggestive of related meanings of memorialisation. Balancing specific signs with enigmatic signifiers kept his project from being read in an entirely aberrant way.

Perhaps, like Gehry, some of his expressive grammar is too often repeated across projects, and his patriotism a little heavy-handed, but one has to applaud his courage in confronting a major problem of the moment: the spiritual crisis, and the loss of a shared metaphysics. Many people, and some philosophers, would say this deprivation in the global age is inevitable and permanent. Yet other philosophers, notably Mary Midgely, argue that new credible, public concepts have emerged, such as the notion of the earth as a self-regulating system, Gaia. The metaphor of a dynamic planet tuning itself through feedback is, of course, one of the insights of the new paradigm in science, but whether architects come up with a public iconography based on Gaia remains to be seen. My belief is that the universe story will become a shared metaphysics and for this reason my own design work is centred around it: various sculptures of DNA, Black Hole Terraces, symmetry breaking structures, a universe cascade, and so forth (pl. 110).[7] Cosmogenesis, the narrative of the underlying process, is not yet a public religion, and may never become one, but it is still more than a diverting pastime of astrophysics. It is the orientation point for the future, in search of a corresponding iconology (that is, an underlying iconography). The Death of God, like the death of other major narratives over the last hundred years, may be confined to the West, especially visible now that the globe is arming for the ultimate clash of civilisations. But fundamentalisms, either American or Other, are not living cultural movements however powerful they may be. They have produced no art, architecture or writing worth preserving, and the deeper problems remain.

In spite of these problems, the question of whether the new paradigm exists in architecture is worth asking. Do these seven strands hold together, does something unite them? Does the Organi-Tech architecture relate to the fractal; do the enigmatic signifiers emerge out of datascapes? Are they connected to the fashion for folding and blob-architecture, the prevalence of landforms and waves; an iconography based on Gaia and cosmogenesis? My view is that the sciences of complexity underlie all these movements, as much as does the computer, while an informing morality has yet to emerge. The answer is mixed. As Nikolaus Pevsner wrote concerning the paradigm of Modernism in nineteenth-century Britain, seven swallows do not necessarily a summer make. True, this may be a false start, the old paradigm of Modernism can easily reassert its hegemony, as it is lurking behind every Bush and Blair. But a wind is stirring architecture; at least it is the beginning of a shift in theory and practice.

For illustrations of this article, the reader is referred to pls. 110-117 and 132.

[1] Santiago Calatrava, City of Arts and Sciences, Valencia, 1991-2002 (pl. 111). Positive organic metaphors but not a fractal grammar. This spectacular urban landscape has many qualities of the new paradigm, and several virtues such as the sculpted white concrete that profiles the structural forces in exciting and innovative ways, but the repetitive nature of the elements typifies the old way of thinking. Much Eco-Tech shows this ambivalent aspect – a half step towards the new paradigm.

[2] Norman Foster, Swiss Re Headquarters, London 1996-2002 (pl. 115). Originally conceived in an egg form, this blob shape was stretched to resemble many other organic things in addition to the notorious gherkin – a pinecone, pineapple, cucumber and phallus – as well as a missile, bullet and bomb. Not only does this polysemy make it an enigmatic signifier, but the computer-perfected entasis makes it a good example of propositional beauty – the central planned skyscraper with elegant double curves shooting to the sky.

[3] Frank Gehry, Guggenheim Bilbao, Bilbao 1993-1997 (pls. 112, 113). The popular and critical success of this building confirmed the enigmatic signifier as the convention for the contemporary monument. Although critics captured part of the suggested overtones of this building – Constructivist artichoke, fish, mermaid and boat – it is the capacity to mean many more things that makes the enigmatic signifier a multivalent symbol. Metaphors drawn by Madelon Vriesendorp.

[4] MvRdV, Dutch Pavilion, Expo 2000, Hanover (pl. 116). A stack of synthetic ecologies and artificial grounds determined as a statistical representation of the future Dutch landscape. From the top down can be found 1) windmills, and water on the artificial lake that flows into 2) sheets of water in an exhibition space and then to 3) a forest grown with high-powered lights. Next level down 4) is an auditorium with projection space, to 5) an agricultural section of smaller plants again artificially lit, to reach 6) a ground floor and grotto of houses and shops. Views and movement are celebrated by the exterior staircase. The sustainability of the closed cycle makes sense, the juxtaposition of gardens and moods is a delight, the remorseless logic humorous, but the question is raised: "Will all of life be managed and pharmed?" No wonder a vocal group in Holland want more wilderness.

[5] FOA, (Moussavi and Zaero-Polo), Yokohama International Port Terminal, 1995-2002 (pl. 114). The landform building as infrastructure and folded landscape of activities. Like the blob building the landform tends to merge floor, wall and roof in a seamless continuity. The architects do not intend the appropriate ship, water and wave metaphors, but like Mies van der Rohe seek a neutral, generic and technological architecture – yet they allow emergence of the unintended.

[6] Daniel Libeskind, Imperial War Museum-North, Trafford, Manchester, 1998-2002 (pl. 117). A symbolic, spiritual and cosmic architecture is still relatively rare but a few architects are trying. Here the globe shattered through conflict is reassembled as three curved shards: the tall Air Shard marks the entrance, and holds flying instruments of war in its open structure; the Earth Shard is a huge exhibition area with even the floor curving gently; the Water Shard curves down towards the adjacent canal and minesweeper moored there. This huge expressive structure is both a giant advertisement, in the sense of Venturi's Duck Building, and an enigmatic signifier of conflict and its resolutions.

[7] Charles Jencks, Universe Cascade, Portrack, Scotland, 2001 (pl. 110). The story of the universe over its 13.7-billion-year history can be understood in broad outlines as jumps in organisation; these are presented here using rocks of various types.

The Virtues of Modernity

ARATA ISOZAKI

I am very pleased to return to Tehran after thirty years, my last visit being in the middle of the 1970s. As a practising architect I have created many different types of buildings over the past forty years, most of them in Japan. I have also written a number of theoretical texts about contemporary architecture and the historical architecture of Europe and Japan. My thoughts in standing in Tehran today turn to the past and present, but also to the best ways to look ahead to the future.

The study of traditional architecture in Japan is increasing, just as Iranians today are interested in their own past. About 150 years ago, Japan started its so-called modernisation. At the beginning of that period we had only traditional Japanese-style architecture that had of course been influenced by China and Korea. In the latter part of the nineteenth century we received strong influences from Europe which were historically oriented buildings born of the Victorian period. Only later did the so-called Modern Movement arrive in Japan. For more than two generations there was a conflict within the country about how to keep some character or specific meaning of traditional Japanese architecture while integrating Modernism.

The middle of the twentieth century brought what we might call the first evidence of globalisation to Japan with the arrival of the International Style of architecture. Again, many Japanese architects debated about the proper way to make use of these trends in our country. The architect Kenzo Tange was my teacher and he actively sought ways of combining modern and Japanese architecture. Many of his aesthetic ideas had to do with Japanese tradition, but he was convinced of the virtues of modernity. With structures like those he designed for the 1964 Tokyo Olympic Games, Kenzo Tange came to be recognised even outside Japan as having created a specifically Japanese version of Modernism. This is when I was starting out as an architect, and it meant that I had to find other directions, to develop other ideas.

Around that time I started studying not only modern architecture but also the history of architecture – traditional Japanese architecture, but also that of Europe. I came to understand the solutions found in different parts of the world in the past and to begin to see relations between these methods. I was determined not to simply follow a modern style, but, by enriching my thoughts with the learning of the past, I sought to create something new. And much of my thought has to do with bringing the past and the present together. I published books about the history of architecture at the same time as I practised as an architect. I became involved in the so-called Metabolist movement of the 1960s that imagined projects related to the future of the city, and its society.

I have heard myself referred to on occasion as a "Post-Modern" architect. If it is true that in the late 1960s I was determined to make constructive use of historical elements, I do not think I really fit into what Charles Jencks called Post-Modernism. My concern with the past was more one of thought than of appearances. How do we define the concept of architecture? I did design some buildings in the 1980s that were published as examples of Post-Modernism, but, again, I sought actively to avoid following any specific style, and to somehow shift the meaning of the elements of architecture. This is what I would call a post-modern way of thinking but not a Post-Modern style of historical quotations.

In the early 1990s information technology began to change our way of designing. Many of my friends, who were indeed of the Post-Modern generation, suffered because they were familiar with what I would call an analogue form of tracing historic elements. They could not keep up with the new trends. Personally this did not pose a problem for me because I did not reuse historical elements in that way. I do have a handwritten design method, but in my office everyone uses computers and my thoughts can be transmitted in this new digital way. Surely we will soon be able to use computers as tools to develop the forms themselves, and this is what I call the process of digitalisation.

I am sure that in Iran many are familiar with my work up through the 1990s. I have chosen to focus more on what I have done in the past three years, in good part through competitions. In competitions, architects are asked to work very rapidly and, despite the aid of the computer, one always lacks the time necessary to fully develop ideas.

A competition I recently lost concerns the Florence Railway Station (pl. 121). The stations in Florence were built in about 1935 under the influence of Mussolini and they are situated on the edge of the town so as to preserve the historic core. A very rapid service has now been laid for Florence and the trains will arrive twenty-five metres underground. The end of the building I proposed was about five hundred metres long and fifty metres wide – like an aircraft carrier. Inspired by the Italian Futurist idea of cars, trains and aircraft in movement, I imagined a sort of airport, a contemporary transportation node conceived around the dynamics of movement (pl. 120). There is a large platform, where helicopters can land and there would be a restaurant with a view of the cathedral and the rest of the city. Because of the height of the building this was strictly limited; the platform was to be sixteen metres high.

For the same city, Florence, I was asked a few years ago by several international architects to make a proposal for the city square and exit from the Uffizi Museum (pls. 122, 123). The Uffizi has significant problems because it was originally designed for the Medici. Now, of course, it serves as a great museum, but it is so popular you have to queue three to four hours to get in. The entrance is one problem, but so is the capacity of the building. The difficulty for the architect is to respond to the historical situation, and at the same time to create a new city square.

I also recently worked on the Caixa Forum in Barcelona, Spain (pls. 124-126). Located near the Barcelona Pavilion designed by Ludwig Mies van der Rohe, this is a contemporary art gallery. Because we could not touch the exterior of that building, my proposal was for an underground gallery with a kind of secret garden with a tree-like structure.

Another recent project concerns a concert hall and a library for Shenzhen, a city with a population of seven million, in China. The concert hall and library would have a common entrance with an atrium supported by four tree-like structures. I used forms that were more geometric than organic for the tree structures, covering one side in gold and the other in silver.

In Doha, the capital of Qatar, we were asked to create a complex containing the national library, a science and natural history museum and a 'space theatre' which is next to the science museum and natural history museum (pls. 127, 128). It is a kind of roofed plaza with four columns supporting the structure. We created this so that spectators would see the fireworks displays that are launched regularly from an island in the bay of Doha. If you look at my earlier work, from the 1960s, you may be familiar with my imaginary project called "The City in the Air". All the city functions would have been set in the sky on a series of columns. When the Emir of Qatar looked at my book and found my city project there he asked me, why not use this idea for the new national library?

And so it seems that ideas continue to live even when we imagine that they are forgotten. It is in the study of architectural tradition that I have found much of the inspiration for my architecture. By looking at the past we learn not to imitate, but if we look more closely, we can see the ideas behind structures – the ways in which they were conceived. That is the real lesson of the past and the way forward to the future.

For projects by Arata Isozaki, the reader is referred to pls. 118-130.

Architecture Now!

PHILIP JODIDIO

What is the situation of contemporary architecture? The question implies a complexity that is far beyond the scope of a brief talk. Where are the most talented architects and what are their styles? Can it be said that there is any dominant style today? The answers to these questions of course vary depending on the part of the world concerned. My recent book, *Architecture Now!*, published in six languages and distributed in seventy countries, attempts an overview of recent buildings and projects originating principally in the Americas, Europe, Japan and Australia. This is not to say that the reality of contemporary architecture is in any way limited to these parts of the world, but it may be fair to say that the exploration of new ideas and techniques is rich enough here to justify interest. The Modernist style born of the Bauhaus, redefined in America and elsewhere, swept across the world after the Second World War, irrespective of many cultural barriers. Today no such force seems to exist, but there are trends dependent on many of the factors that have traditionally influenced architecture. The demands of a site, of a client, the function of a building, one might be tempted to say its ambitions — all of these are elements that can give rise to different solutions, some of which are exemplary. I would like to politely disagree with some of the ideas expressed here in the paper by Charles Jencks. He suggested that architects are trying strenuously to integrate some kind of undefined but nonetheless complex new world view into their work. Obviously if our entire view of the universe changes, then architects may have to rethink their ideas about reaching only for the moon.

While we wait for that event, it seems clear that architects will think rather of such issues as cost, site, function and the poor forgotten user of their buildings before moving on to the higher issues of cosmogenesis and "strange attractors". Yes, architects can and do think of our place in the universe, but the new directions of architecture can certainly not be classified according to a grand scheme. Nor can we be so simplistic as to say that Modernism was born of a purely mechanistic view of existence. Einstein's Theory of Relativity, Heisenberg's Uncertainty Principle, emerged years before Modernist boxes began their inexorable march around the world. Architecture and science may not always go hand in hand. Fortunately, trends in architecture are more unexpected and varied than any critic's attempt to assign them to a new order, no matter how imprecise. Yes, architecture is changing, but rather than a new paradigm, there is a new freedom, a new diversity.

Many of those who follow architecture might tell you that the current style looks much like Frank Gehry's Experience Music Project, completed in Seattle, Washington, four years ago (pl. 131). If you look at this image and find that it brings to mind Gehry's Bilbao Guggenheim, easily the most published and talked about building of the 1990s, you are absolutely right. Frank Gehry, undoubtedly the most sculptural of today's major architects cites his sources with no shame. In his 1989 acceptance speech for the Pritzker Prize, he said: "My artist friends, like Jasper Johns, Bob Rauschenberg, Ed Kienholz and Claes Oldenburg, were working with very inexpensive materials – broken wood and paper – and they were making beauty. These were not superficial details, they were direct, and raised the question in my mind of what beauty was. I chose to use the craft available, and to work with craftsmen and make a virtue out of their limitations. Painting had an immediacy that I craved for in architecture. I explored the process of new construction materials to try to give feeling and spirit to form. In trying to find the essence of my own expression, I fantasised that I was an artist standing before a white canvas deciding what the first move should be."

One of the most surprising and ambitious of Frank O. Gehry's recent buildings, the ten thousand-square-metre Experience Music Project was financed in good part by Microsoft co-founder Paul Allen. At a cost of $240 million, it became a constructive response to I. M. Pei's Cleveland Rock and Roll Hall of Fame (1995), although it was originally intended to house only Allen's collection of Jimi Hendrix memorabilia. Clad in aluminium and stainless steel panels, the building features a use of colour that is unusual in Gehry's work. The choice of colours was inspired by rock and roll or guitar themes such as blue for Fender, gold for Les Paul and purple for Jimi Hendrix's song, "Purple Haze". Gehry adds that the red passages are a tribute to the faded old trucks rock and roll stars used to drive. One source of the architect's inspiration for the forms was the idea of a shattered 1960s' Fender Stratocaster guitar, yet the whole retains the kind of abstract, sculptural volumes that made him world-famous in Bilbao. Here, as in Spain, Gehry made use of computer assisted design on a large scale, feeding images of guitars into the imaging software and morphing them almost beyond recognition. Each of the building's twenty-one thousand panels has a unique shape and size and is cut and bent to fit exactly in its specific location. Gehry insists on the conviviality of the design, saying: "With its folds, the building is intended to be huggable, like a mother cradling a baby in her arms against the folds of her garment."

Others have willingly followed in the footsteps of Frank Gehry, adding an artistic element to their architectural expression. One of these is a younger Californian architect named Eric Owen Moss, a talented designer whose work is concentrated in the Los Angeles area of Culver City. His Umbrella Building is, like other former warehouses he has renovated, unusual mainly because of the architect's sculptural intervention near the entrance area. The Umbrella is a 1,470-square-metre project undertaken for a cost of $1,185,000. It is made up of two contiguous warehouses built in the 1940s, renovated to include twenty private offices, two conference areas and large open workspaces. The name of the "Umbrella" comes from what Moss calls "an experimental piece of construction". "It is a conceptual bowl," he says, "an arena the slope of which is determined by the curving top chord of two inverted wood trusses salvaged from the demolition of an adjacent project and inserted here." Like most of his Culver City projects, this renovation does not fundamentally alter the exterior forms of the existing structures. Rather Moss chooses to add a sculptural element whose origin is linked to the spaces. It is this added piece that gives an unusual identity to the completed building, and appeals to possible occupants.

Obviously the sculptural or artistic interventions of talented architects like Frank Gehry or Eric Owen Moss add something to buildings, but is there fundamentally any innovation involved? A pretty building draws clients or visitors in the case of a museum, but does it really advance architecture very much? Frank Gehry is said to be complaining that since he built the Guggenheim Bilbao, all his clients want him to do buildings of that type. He is a victim of his own success, trapped in a style. With its references to anthropomorphic sources such as the "mother cradling a baby", or flowers, fish and horse heads, Gehry's work does in some sense come closer to art than it does to a really new type of architecture. The "horse-head" that inspired his conference room for the new DG Bank in Berlin was first exhibited in a smaller scale version at the Gagosian Art Gallery in Beverly Hills California.

Another significant figure of contemporary architecture, Zaha Hadid recently completed her first built works after establishing a considerable reputation based on her drawings, and indeed on her personality. Her design for the so-called Mind Zone under the Millennium Dome, in Greenwich, England, was not intended as a piece of permanent architecture, but rather as a temporary exhibition pavilion under the Dome designed by Richard Rogers. Situated in the midst of the circus-type atmosphere of the Millennium Dome, Zaha Hadid's Mind Zone stood out with its spectacular cantilevered steel structure. As the designer said: "Our minds are amazingly complex machines and our aim was to unravel some of their mysteries in a truly memorable fashion." Working with a number of talented artists such as Ron Mueck, Gavin Turk and Richard Deacon, Hadid indeed succeeded in creating spaces that appeared to defy gravity and to prepare the visitor for the technologically oriented exhibits within the pavilion. A well-designed circus attraction? Why not.

The borders between art and architecture have been intentionally stretched by a number of people in recent years. Maya Lin, perhaps best known in the United States for the Vietnam War Memorial she designed in Washington in 1981, is a rare case in that she is more recognised as an artist than as an architect. Her Langston Hughes Library, completed in Knoxville, Tennessee, in 1999, is based on a hundred-year-old cantilevered Tennessee barn that she literally took apart and set up on two support cribs. The library space, measuring about one hundred square metres, is the single upper-level room whose surfaces are clad in maple, beige carpet and brown recycled particleboard. Set on a farm owned by the Children's Defense Fund, the inside of this library has little relation to the rough-hewn timber of the barn — a fact that has led to criticism of Maya Lin. She compares the design to a "diamond in the rough". "When you cut into it," she says, "it reveals a more polished inner self."

Using art and architecture to commercial ends has become a very active area in the United States, Europe or Japan. One of the cleverest approaches to this synthesis of art and money has been Rei Kawakubo, the head of the Comme des Garçons label in Japan. Her Flagship Store in Tokyo existed previously to its 1999 renovation, but she called on numerous artists and architects to give it a very particular appearance. The undulating glass façade was designed by the English group Future Systems. This shop is set on the same street, Omote Sando, where Tadao Ando built his Collezione boutique building some years ago and where a new Prada shop is being completed by Herzog and De Meuron from Switzerland. Architecture and fashion here converge, and the design contributes to setting out the image that Comme des Garçons wishes to project — an image that goes beyond clothing.

New architecture, especially of the innovative type, is often driven by the desire to make money. Museums must attract tourists, shops need buyers. What better way to draw in the crowds than to give an artistic or unusual appearance to a design? Making money or drawing attention are certainly two of the contemporary functions of architecture, but fortunately not the only ones.

Economic constraints have also driven architects in recent years to seek out an aesthetic that is inspired by early Modernism and also by Minimalism in art. Factory or warehouse design has long interested talented engineers and architects, and the Dutchman Wiel Arets with his Lensvelt Factory and Offices, in Breda, the Netherlands, is no exception (pl. 135). Consisting of a warehouse, office, showroom and assembly area, this facility for a furniture manufacturer is set in an industrial park. With a floor area of about 6,500 square metres, and a height of eight metres, the double-glazed structure is intended to glow from within after nightfall. The vertical glass panels are attached to the steel frame only at mid-height, giving an impression of simplicity and transparency to the whole. A cantilevered opaque metal box set just above two metres off the ground on the east side of the building houses a conference room. A similar box, located much closer to the ground on the west side marks the main entrance and employees' lounge. Between these two opaque volumes, an interior courtyard offers access to two symmetrical showrooms. Corrugated metal roofing material also forms the inside ceiling of the warehouse, while a simple concrete floor accentuates the intelligent, minimalist design.

Minimalism has also been popular with architects who dispose of very considerable means, such as the Japanese master Yoshio Taniguchi with his Gallery of Horyuji Treasures at the Tokyo National Museum (pl. 138). This new structure by the architect selected to rebuild the Museum of

Modern Art in New York was designed to house a number of works originally from the Horyuji Temple in Nara. The building covers an area of 1,934 square metres and has a total floor area of four thousand square metres. It is a four-storey structure built of reinforced concrete with a steel frame. Inspired by the wooden boxes used to protect precious art objects in Japan, the design includes a high metal canopy, a glazed entrance area and a completely darkened inner exhibition area. Open on two sides to the garden environment with a shallow basin marking the entrance area, this building has a jewel-like precision in its construction. It is a masterpiece in itself, worthy of one of the finest architects currently working in Japan.

Another Japanese architect who has reached with success into the traditions of Modernism to create a powerful body of work that also has its roots in Japan, is Tadao Ando. Ando recently completed what might in some ways be considered his masterwork, the so-called Awaji Yumebutai on the Island of Awaji not far from the cities of Kobe and Osaka (pl. 133). The site is unusual in that it had been completely laid bare during work on the Kansai International Airport. Earth and sand removed from here were used for the landfill of the artificial island on which the airport is built and for other artificial islands in the region over a period of thirty years. The challenge for the architect was not only to build structures, but also to "regenerate nature from the devastated ground". Fortunately, the warm, humid climate means that nature quickly reclaims the land, but Tadao Ando's ambition was far greater than this. As he describes it: "The programme is for a multi-use facility including a botanical garden, a place for the study of horticulture, an open air theatre, a convention hall, a hotel and a guest house. Our first idea was to restore the greenery, more specifically to hold a flower exhibition there and to develop the area into a permanent garden. We called this the 'Millennium Garden', and the project was developed on the basis of that concept. It was decided that the facilities would be linked by living things, that is, plants such as trees and flowers, and the flow of water and people. The Alhambra in Grenada provides a historical model. There, water links small patios together." What is most striking about the Awaji Yumebutai is the progression of sonorous, beautiful architectural and garden spaces outside the buildings themselves.

Another established master has dealt with the wealth of Modernist tradition in different ways, based on his Portuguese origins. Alvaro Siza recently completed a new building for the Serralves Foundation, in his native city of Porto, Portugal (pl. 139). The Foundation was created through a partnership between the Portuguese government and fifty private sector partners. Established in the Quinta de Serralves, a large property including a main house built in the 1930s located not far from the centre of Porto, the Foundation specialises in contemporary art. Siza's new structure, located in the park of the Foundation is both substantial in size and ambitious in scope. Using a suspended ceiling system similar to the one he devised for the Galician Centre of Contemporary Art, Siza created a number of large, flexible galleries, intended for temporary shows. Internal courtyards and numerous windows permit the visitor to remain in contact with the attractive park environment (three hectares of which Siza is responsible for).

Though less directly inspired by early twentieth-century masters, Norman Foster in England has carried forward an international career that is now bringing him his first very visible London commissions. His Greater London Authority headquarters is located on the Thames near Tower Bridge, directly opposite the Tower of London. This new ten-storey structure has about fifteen thousand square metres of available floor space and was built for a cost of approximately £40 million. An office for the Lord Mayor of London and the Cabinet are located on the eighth floor of this "flask-like form". The unusual spherical shape of the building "has been generated as a result of thorough scientific analysis, aiming to reduce both solar gain and heat loss via the building's skin, thus reducing the building's energy needs". More specifically, energy consumption is to be reduced to twenty-five percent of a typical air-conditioned office requirement. Beyond the specific building concerned here, Foster's GLC headquarters illustrates the trend to use new, often computer-driven design methods to create architecture with surprising new shapes. Foster is certainly in tune with the environmental impact of his work, but it could be argued that an unusual shape serves little other purpose than to be noticed more.

Despite events such as the September 11 attack in New York, tall buildings remain another area of significant urban presence for architects. China's rapid economic expansion has brought forth the desire, if not the need to construct skyscrapers of record height. The American architects Kohn Pederson Fox have designed the Shanghai World Financial Centre intended, at 460 metres in height, to be the tallest building in the world when it is completed in 2004. Located in the Financial and Trade District in Pudong, the building's most spectacular feature, apart from its height, is the fifty-metre cylindrical void at the top, baptised the "moon gate". This opening, which gives the tower something of the appearance of an archaic Chinese artefact, serves to relieve wind pressure on the structure. To contain office and retail space as well as a hotel, the tower's form is based on the intersection of a square prism and a cylinder. Retail space will be housed in the lower, podium area, and the building will rise to a total of ninety-five storeys, clearly marking the emergence of China in general, and Shanghai in particular, as economic forces to be reckoned with. Another building that desires to be noticed.

Economic concerns coupled with a certain respect for the recent architectural past have made the renovation of twentieth-century buildings a new and very popular area of intervention for talented architects. One of the most spectacular initiatives of this type was of course the new Tate Modern in London by Herzog and De Meuron. Located opposite St Paul's Cathedral on the Thames, the Bankside Power Station was built in two phases, in 1947 and 1963, by Sir Giles Gilbert Scott, who was also the inventor of the famous red English telephone cabin. Shut down in 1981 because it was polluting London too much, the Bankside Power Plant is dominated by a ninety-nine-metre-high chimney, visible from much of inner London. The Tate Gallery took an option on the purchase of the building in 1994, and organised a competition the following year that selected Herzog and De Meuron as architects, over the likes of Tadao Ando, Rem Koolhaas, and Renzo Piano. Preserving the spectacular space of the former Turbine Hall as the entrance area, the Swiss architects opted for an approach that conserves the rough, industrial qualities of the building, while providing ten thousand square metres of state-of-the-art exhibition space on the Thames side of the building. Polished concrete and rough cut wood alternate on the floor surfaces, and numerous viewpoints permit visitors to orient themselves *vis-à-vis* the Thames and the Turbine Hall. A rather harsh florescent lighting scheme might appear to be the only obvious fault of this ambitious project. With over five million visitors in its first year of operation, Tate Modern is regarded a considerable success.

Another renovation of a very different type was carried out by the Californian architects Marmol and Radziner on the iconic Kaufmann House located in Palm Springs. Originally designed in 1946 by the architect Richard Neutra, this house was built for the same client who commissioned Frank Lloyd Wright's Falling Water. As the house had been significantly modified by successive owners since its construction, Marmol and Radziner set out to return it to its original state. Approximately three hundred square metres in size at the outset, the house had been expanded to almost five hundred square metres. These later additions were done away with. One of the key elements in the restoration was the use of Julius Shulman's famous 1947 photographs of the house. The architects decided to return the garden to the indigenous desert landscape that existed in Neutra's time. Neutra's minimalism is considered by many to be particularly significant today, when there has been a return to such pared down simplicity. Far from the billowing curves of Frank Gehry's California dream, Neutra's pure straight lines seem particularly refreshing today.

Where renovation was not the client's desire, other designers have succeeded in bringing contemporary architecture closer to a real symbiosis with an existing historical environment. Contrary to the idea of the *tabula rasa* that haunted early Modernism, this is a modernity that lives with its environment. An example of this type of concept is Rafael Moneo's Murcia Town Hall in Spain. Situated on the Cardinal Belluga Plaza, near a cathedral and the Cardinal's Palace, this is a three thousand-square-metre building. Rafael Moneo had the difficult task of creating a building that neither challenged the architectural power of the older structures, nor timidly denied contemporary municipal power. The reinforced concrete Town Hall is clad in local sandstone and brick. Interior finishes are in plaster, wood panelling, with stone and wood floors. The programme required space for the municipal offices, a tourist and information centre, lecture hall, reception room and cafeteria. As Rafael Moneo says: "The façade is organised like a musical score, numerically accepting the horizontal levels of the floor slabs. It resists symmetries and offers as the key element the balcony of the gallery that rests on exactly the same horizontal plane as the central balcony of the *piano nobile* of the Palace, both at the same height."

In a world where architecture is commanded largely by money, it may be useful to recall that some talented architects use their skills to seek out real innovations that may sometimes benefit those who are not well-off, as opposed to the fortunate users of most of the buildings shown here today. Toshiko Mori, recently named Chairman of the Department of Architecture at Harvard has indeed thought about a less glamorous side of her profession that may be far more important than the glitter of fashion. Her "Woven Inhabitation" presented at the Artists' Space in New York in 1999 seeks to provide a simple, elegant solution to the vast problem of providing temporary housing to refugees or victims of natural disasters. Her concept is to make use of "the woven remnants of revolutionary industrial fabrics already utilised by the aerospace, medical and fashion industries but never before developed as architectural building products". Mori proposes an elegant, inexpensive solution to a vast problem.

Another Japanese born architect, Shigeru Ban has thought extensively about the creation of shelters made for the homeless out of... paper. Ban has demonstrated amply that if properly treated, paper can be used as a structural element. His Japanese Pavilion for Expo 2000 in Hanover, Germany (pl. 134), was made of recycled paper tubes as the primary structural material. The foundation was designed using temporary rental scaffolding, stones and sand in order to minimise construction costs and to aid in reuse of the materials. Despite his use of the paper tube technique in Japan and its approval for structural uses by Japanese authorities, Shigeru Ban had never attempted such a large-scale structure before and, as such, he called on the assistance of the noted light-architecture specialist Frei Otto.

In a fundamental way, seeking to use paper as a structural material could be seen as a challenge to the myth of solidity that has always surrounded architecture. Plainly said, many of today's architects, and particularly the younger ones, do not conceive of their work as being intended to last for centuries, or even decades. Like some artists, they have sought to dissolve walls and open spaces in new ways. One of the most poetic efforts of this type was successfully carried out by the New York architects Diller and Scofidio for the Swiss national Expo 02 on the banks of the lake of Neuchâtel at Yverdon. This structure was intended to resemble nothing so much as a cloud hovering over the lake. Ninety metres wide, sixty metres deep, nine metres thick and rising to fifty metres above the water, the 'cloud' effect was obtained through the use of filtered lake water "shot as a fine mist through a dense array of high-pressure water nozzles integrated into a large cantilevered structure". A ramp lead into the cloud where visitors discover a sort of sensory deprivation due to the "white-out" accompanied by "white noise" related to the mist projectors.

Many younger architects across the world have of course begun in significant ways to use computer assisted design in their work. Beyond the practical considerations of normal construction, some seek to design buildings that will never exist anywhere else but on a computer screen. An example of this trend is Asymptote's Virtual Guggenheim Museum (pls. 136, 137). As part of a larger project intended to commission Internet based works of art, the Guggenheim Museum in New York has asked Asymptote to create the "first important virtual building of the twenty-first century," a fusion of "information space, art, commerce and architecture". This ambitious plan, calling for "navigable three dimensional spatial entities accessible on the Internet as well as a real time interactive component installed at the various Guggenheim locations," imagines a virtual architecture that would change with visitor preferences or uses. In this sense, the Virtual Guggenheim will be in constant flux, corresponding, according to the architects, to the real requirements of truly contemporary art and art appreciation. The economic difficulties of the Guggenheim have at least temporarily put a hold on the full development of this particular project, but virtual buildings are nonetheless very much a part of the present and future of architecture.

The Dutch group MvRdV created a video installation for the Stroom Centre for the Visual Arts in The Hague at the end of 1998 (pl. 132). Their "Metacity/Datatown" is essentially an exhibition that has been shown in such locations as Glasgow's Lighthouse. "Datatown," say the architects, "is based only upon data. It is a city that wants to be described by information; a city that knows no given topography, no prescribed ideology, no representation, no context." Extrapolating from the rapid expansion of urban centres, based on methods of transportation and communication, MvRdV concludes that the Datatown of the future will measure some four hundred kilometres square (roughly the distance from Tokyo to Osaka), and that it will have an extremely high population density (1,477 inhabitants per square kilometre) that would imply a city population of 241 million people. A cross between computer games such as Sim City and genuine urban development ideas, Metacity/Datatown is also an aesthetic environment that reflects the design thinking of this influential Dutch firm, even if the world is not quite ready for the 376 Datatowns they imagine (in other words, a world urban population of more than eighty-eight billion persons).

Returning at last after this very rapid and selective overview of some recent buildings and projects, to the more 'real' world, is the French architect Jean Nouvel's plan for the new Museum of Arts and Civilisations, in Paris, scheduled for 2004 completion if all goes well. Jean Nouvel's project was chosen as a result of an international competition whose original fifteen participants, including Tadao Ando, MvRdV, and Rem Koolhaas, were narrowed down to three (Nouvel, Renzo Piano and Peter Eisenman) early in December 1999. Working with the noted landscape architect Gilles Clément and the lighting expert Yann Kersalé, Nouvel proposed a 7,500-square-metre garden on the 2.5-hectare lot situated on the banks of the River Seine. The main building will be two hundred metres long and will be set twelve metres off the ground. Two smaller structures will house logistical facilities and a media centre. Working with Françoise Raynaud on this project, Nouvel promises to pay careful attention to ecological concerns, making ample usage of materials that can be recycled. The museum will house collections coming from the Musée de l'Homme and the Musée des Arts d'Afrique et d'Océanie. For all of his recent projects, Nouvel has used this type of computer perspective to translate a style that appears to change with each new project.

Nouvel's lack of apparent style, or his willingness to change approaches based on each new project are indicative in a fundamental way of a real current trend in contemporary architecture. The only real style is no style. Architects have assimilated the conquests of early Modernism and gone beyond into the new realms offered by the computer, for example. Much contemporary architecture is influenced by questions of money and being noticed. This does not mean that it must necessarily be considered a superficial pursuit, although the tendency of architects to take themselves for artists does not always auger well for the users, for the people who must live with buildings that remain fashionable for just a year or two. Would it be surprising to say that some of the most potentially interesting buildings seen here today are made of cloth, paper and mist?

Established architects such as Rafael Moneo in Spain, Alvaro Siza in Portugal or Tadao Ando in Japan have adapted the lessons of modern architecture to their own countries. This lesson need not be lost because science makes progress in other areas, nor will restorations of buildings stop. From the sculptural approach of the (aging) Californians to the Minimalism of the Dutch or Japanese, from the dissolving walls of buildings made of water mist, to the virtual reality of structures not intended ever to be built, architecture now is alive and well, embracing diversity, refusing easy classification.

Perhaps a time of economic austerity will mean more attention to those who use buildings, though many of these works of architecture make the spirit soar and open the mind. That realisation may also be what contemporary architecture is all about.

For illustrations of this article, the reader is referred to pls. 131-139.

Eco-Design and Planning

KEN YEANG

I am going to talk about the work that I have been doing for the last twenty years: trying to design ecological buildings and masterplans. I call this designing artificial ecosystems, because this is basically what I am trying to do.

This is a brick; I am showing an image of a brick because it is important to realise that most of the buildings that we design are inorganic. In fact if you look at the building we are in, the Tehran Museum of Contemporary Art, everything in it is inorganic, except you and me and the bugs. So the biggest question that occurred to me is: "Where is the organic component?" When people talk about green buildings, where is the greenery? For me, if we are to look at green buildings or ecological buildings at this most fundamental level of understanding it is necessary to bring more greenery into them, and to balance the abiotic constituents with the biotic as with ecosystems in nature.

In 1986, we realised a building for IBM with planting running continuously up the façade. The greenery starts from a patch at ground level and then goes upwards, around the corner, and makes its way to the top of the building.

Being based in Malaysia we are of course more used to the conditions that arise close to the equator, but we also work in London, which is fifty-two degrees above the equator. There, the sun falls mostly on the south façade, and so the greenery is planted essentially on the south, south-east and south-west facing surfaces. There are a number of features that we have learned about putting vegetation in buildings. For instance, it is important to choose hardy species that are specific to the locality, especially non-flowering ones that survive well in winter and summer. The resistant kinds of species that grow spontaneously near railroads and as hedges along roadsides are the kinds that we try to select for tall buildings.

In ecology, an ecosystem consists of organic and inorganic components, acting as a whole. Nature consists of physical components, both inorganic and organic. If you think about it for a minute, what we as human beings are doing is making the environment of the world more and more inorganic, and more artificial. We build roads, we build bridges, we build buildings, we build marinas making the biospheres more and more concrete, artificial and inorganic. We are also destroying our forests, so the biosphere is being simplified; its complexity and biodiversity are being drastically reduced. If I were to leave a single thought with you when you leave this room today it would be to bring more greenery and organic mass into your buildings.

I started to look at different ways of putting greenery into the built environment. We can either put it all in one place, or put the biomass in a series of locations in a pattern of patches that may or may not be integrated with each other. Ecologically it is better to have an integrated continuous pattern so that different species can interact or migrate, creating a much more diversified and stable ecosystem.

You can have series of green courts or squares, you can have a spine, or you can have a series of corridors with fingers, or even a network. These last two are the preferred patterns that serve as guidelines for me, when I do my master planning and architectural design work.

When I look at a site for the first time I usually ask myself what sort of site it is. Is it an ecologically mature site, like a pine or rain-forest, or is it ecologically immature, which is to say a site that is partially devastated by man? It could be a mixed artificial site, where there is a combination of man-made and natural elements, like a park. It could be a monoculture site like an agricultural field, a corn field. Or is it a city-centre site, where there are no natural components at all, neither flora nor fauna?

From the monoculture to the ecologically mature site it is necessary to do a thorough ecological analysis before you start putting buildings on it. Obviously the complexity of the ecological analysis depends on the site. Any ecosystem is very complex; it can be compared to the human body. A real ecological analysis cannot be done in a day, a week or a month; a full year is required. That is the time it takes to see the energy and material flows, and the species diversity, and so on.

We, as architects, and designers, and engineers, usually do not have the luxury of time. So in the 1960s landscape architects developed what they called a layer-cake method for looking at an ecosystem. Any site is regarded as being made up of a series of layers and you can map each of the layers to study the ecosystem. It is very easy to look at this statistically, but for each of these layers the interactions tend to be very complex. So it is more than just mapping – you have to understand the inter-layer relationships as well. After you map the layers, you overlay them and assign points and then produce a composite map to help you in the location and shaping of your building.

I started to look at the way species move across cities. In a city, even though it is very well developed, you may have patches of green here and there. Some species are able to migrate across urban areas. Such movement may only be gradual – it does not happen in one or two years but may require sixty or eighty years in a city.

I started to talk to my ecological designer friends and I asked them what ecological design is. For many, ecological design is construction with minimal impact on the environment. I said to myself, isn't that a dreadful way of looking at designing, because even if you try to design with as little detrimental impact as possible, you will always have an impact on the environment. It is a receding battle you will never win. So I thought about how we could design to have a positive, rather than negative, impact on the environment, as a much more positive and cheerful proposition My response was to design in order to help increase biodiversity.

Let us say we have two sites, A and B, divided by a road or a highway that inhibits species migration and interaction. Now consider what happens if we bridge the road and make the bridge wide enough and have it vegetated so as to provide opportunities for species to interact and migrate. In this way we contribute to improving the biodiversity of the site and improve its connectivity, rather than trying to avoid reducing the biodiversity.

For a master plan we did in Quanzhou, in China, this was exactly our planning strategy. We designed the whole scheme with interconnecting vegetation, from one end of the site to the other, and we created a series of landscape bridges to cross some of the main roads across the site.

I get increasingly distressed every time I pick up a magazine and some architect talks about the fact that he has designed an ideal ecological building. The reason why I feel distressed is because we are a long way from being able to design a truly ecological building. Most magazines have the idea that if you assemble enough eco-gadgets such as solar collectors, photovoltaics, and recycling systems in one single building, then you have ecological architecture. The result may be a low-energy building, but is it really an ecological building?

Architects and scientists today can calculate the embodied energy in a building. For instance a typical office building would require between eleven and sixteen giga-joules per square metre.

Any building also has an operational cost. It uses energy to operate. Then we need to consider the end costs which must include demolition, reuse and recycling because you have to take into account what happens with that building at the end of its useful life. It uses huge amounts of energy and materials, and has people using the building, which has transport consequences. It also gives up a huge amount of energy. All these factors are interconnected.

I would like to talk about the operational systems in a building, because, to me, buildings are basically enclosures for some human or human-related activity. It may be for office use, for entertainment, a residence, or even a warehouse, but it is basically an enclosure produced by human beings for some sort of activity. The enclosure is built to protect us from the elements. In modern times we have mechanical electrical systems that use energy and materials. Essentially there are four modes to create comfort conditions in buildings. The first one is passive, the second is mixed, the third is full, and the fourth is the productive mode.

The passive mode is basically a building which has no mechanical electrical systems, such as in traditional buildings in any country in the world. Passive mode design takes into account the climate of a place without any electro-mechanical effort to improve conditions. The mixed mode uses some mechanical-electrical systems, such as ceiling fans, or double-skin walls, and so on. The third mode is in fact any conventional building you see; it will have full electro-mechanical systems. In the productive mode, a structure generates some of its own energy through photovoltaics, for example.

When you are designing a building it is necessary to first optimise all passive mode strategies, before you go to mixed or to full mode. This is also a sensible way of looking at design, because if your building is designed to optimise the passive mode, it remains comfortable even without external energy. If you have not optimised your passive mode strategy, then if, for instance, there is no electricity and no external energy source, the building becomes intolerable to use.

We designed another building for the IBM franchise building in 1992 (which received an Aga Khan Award) with some passive strategies (pl. 95). We mapped the sun path of the locality, so the first strategy was in shaping the configuration so that the hot sides of the building are buffered by the elevator cores. We made diagrams optimising all the passive mode strategies heading towards a low energy situation.

A full mode building would probably use anything between 100 and 400 Kw/h per square metre per annum. In the United Kingdom as a temperate climate, it is held that a good benchmark is to try to achieve 100 Kw/h per square metre per annum for commercial buildings. If we use mixed mode, like for instance in Tehran where you have a cold winter and a hot summer, because of the humidity level you can use evacuative cooling as a mixed mode system.

If you insist on having consistent temperature throughout the year, then you have a full mode situation. If you are prepared to be a little colder in winter and a little hotter in summer, then you are heading towards a low energy situation.

We have recently designed a building in Malaysia which is naturally ventilated, meaning that it uses wind to create conditions of comfort. This is an example of how a developing nation can cope with the very real problems posed by excessive energy consumption.

There are architects who first consider the ecosystem, such as myself, and others who approach these problems from the engineering end. There are fundamental differences between the two ways of working, because where I start with nature and ecology, the opposite approach begins with technology. There are many engineering-driven architects who tend to start with pre-established specifications. We look for systemic integration, where engineers look for system efficiency. One is artificial, the other is natural. The big problem is how to design our buildings in a more natural manner.

My opinion is that we should concentrate our design efforts towards looking at the interface between natural systems and our man-made systems. An architect is really the one who should try to design artificial systems that can form a mechanically and organically integrated whole. In many ways it is just like designing a prosthetic device. All of us are designing buildings that are artificial, prosthetic devices, which we somehow have to integrate with the host organic system – which is nature, the biosphere – and with the ecosystems.

The environmental integration that we seek between our man-made systems and the natural systems in nature is not just mechanical but organic; for example, in the case of an artificial heart. If you take the most advanced artificial heart that we can produce, it still uses external energy sources. It uses batteries. We are still unable to develop an artificial heart that uses the energy of the body. Furthermore, the survival rate is seventy percent. So if we cannot even design an artificial prosthetic device to interface in a truly organic and self-sustaining way, then can you imagine how far we are from being able to design an ecological architecture that can truly integrate with all the systems in nature?

I started here by looking at the properties of ecosystems and how we could re-interpret them in our man-made world. I do believe in principle that today we are able to achieve all of this technologically but have not yet begun to do so in effective and efficient ways.

What should an ecological building look like? What is the ecological aesthetic? My early work was very mechanical, and my later work is much more organic. At the end of the day, I think that a design's benign systemic integration with the natural environment is the most important aspect of eco-design.

For projects by Ken Yeang, the reader is referred to pls. 95, 96 and 140-147.

Eleven Tasks for Urban Design

MICHAEL SORKIN

Urban design is a rump. Founded in a vacated crack between architecture and planning, its aim was to rescue physical urbanism from the humongous onus of 'planning'. Not an unreasonable aim. The yoking of the roughshod therapies of urban renewal with the enervated stylings of Modernism – the double culmination of the long march of a universalism that had long since lost its way – had, by the 1960s, given planners a permanently bad name. Like the craven lie of Vietnam, the decimation wreaked on neighbourhoods 'for their own good' exposed a contradiction that could not but collapse the structures that produced it.

Ironically, the critique came simultaneously from opposing directions. Progressives – including locally-based 'advocacy' planners – attacked the juggernaut of command urbanism, exposed its anti-democratic, racist assumptions, and sought to empower local communities. The preservationism of the 1960s and 1970s was galvanised as an oppositional practice, in defence of homes and neighbourhoods threatened by highways, urban renewal, and development. Its stewardship of the existing urban fabric opposed homogenising solutions by establishing a link between life and place, defending the complex, elusive, ecologies of neighbourhood against the one-dimensional fantasies of the planners.

While this fight for community control was being waged politically, a second, more purely formal critique was launched from the camp of the Post-Modernists who assailed Modernist architecture not simply as the expression of the planners' disciplinary designs but as their source. With its reflexive venerations of tradition and its preferences for historical stylings and the forms of the pre-industrial city, architectural Post-Modernism was undergirded by a very different set of political assumptions than those of progressive preservationists. Implicitly and often explicitly, this backward-looking urbanism evoked and celebrated the putative social relations of 'simpler' times, a monochrome, paternalistic vision of unalienated labour in an unpressured environment: Reaganville. But this Post-Modernist nostalgia participated in the same fallacy which doomed the Modernism it sought to displace: conflating principles with forms, it both imputed superior virtue to particular styles and insisted that architecture was the answer. As the only vigorous and 'new' argument available about the form of the city, though, this neo-conservative, historicist, view swept the field, rapidly becoming the default paradigm for academic urban design.

Part of the legacy of the oppositional origins of citizen participation and neighbourhood preservationism is a generalised fear of physical models. Decades of well-rehearsed critiques of the Master Plan have resulted in a kind of baby-with-the-bathwaterism, in a reticence of vision. While many fine designs have been conceived for the refitting of neighbourhoods based on empowerment, sustainability, pedestrianism, or post-Daddy-Mummy-and-Me domesticity, few projects for that transcend received models have been formulated. Today, the field is dominated by the rejiggered suburbanism of the so-called 'new' urbanists. The far more promising – indeed crucial – sensibility of environmentalism is hemmed by its almost complete lack of a constituency among architects, planners (and politicians) and by its corollary failure to produce a critical mass of legible urbanistic innovation.

This must be reversed. Our existing cities need gentle (and rapid) retrofitting with an elaborating apparatus of sustainability, with gardens and solar collectors, with ecological construction, with traffic-free streets and neighbourhoods made over by the algorithms of walk-time. But this is not enough: too often, green models are themselves propositions about decay, about allowing the contemporary city to decompose until it reacquires the character of the historic one, another style of preservationism. While it is crucial, of course, to nurture the best parts of our cities, the vital neighbourhoods and the climax forms, these tasks cannot delimit the agenda of an urbanism that truly looks to the future. Fixated on the historical city as a source for its own inventions, urban design today both blinkers itself against the emergence of marvellous new architectures and largely resists coming to grips with urbanism's greatest crisis, the crazy, disastrous, explosion of the fringe. Subject to abundant critique that never rises above itself, the edge city remains an imaginative wasteland, uncomprehended by designers who – fixated on historical patterns as both the locus and boiler-plate for their research – give themselves over to monofuntional enclavism and the rarefactions of pure nostalgia.

Urban design is ready for an explosion of fresh forms, inspired by the democratic roots of the critique of modernist urbanism, by a deeply ecological sensibility, by a fond embrace of the pluralist character of our culture, and by a critical incorporation of the new and inescapably transformative technologies of electronic adjacency. This will lead not simply to the evolution of existing urban centres but must inevitably also result in the construction of many entirely new cities. A world population growing exponentially and our wounded biosphere demand no less. Urban design needs to escape the comfortable mire of mastery over forms and circumstances long ago learned: restoring existing cities to their original scales and patterns is no longer a fundamental problem for the architectural imagination, however thorny such a project may be socially, politically, or economically.

We suffer such a poverty of vision. Urban design can provide a remedy by cultivating numerous fresh fantasies of urban desirability, happy futures which exceed the mindful simplicities of both modernism and historicism to produce places of ravishing complexity. For this, we need the most dedicated and optimistic research. Without it, our cities will simply recycle themselves into increasingly ersatz locales, Disneylands of disconnect between form and meaning, scenes of architectural rituals that grow emptier and emptier. Without it, our cities will choke on their own waste, subject to ever more dire forms of collapse as they grow too far beyond comprehension and tractability.

While there can never be – should never be – a single architectural answer to the form of the city, there must be a complicit set of principles governing the urban project, principles which inform but do not finalise the myriad individuations that must become the goal of a revitalised urban design practice. Even as we revere the glorious legacies of thousands of years of successful urbanism, the struggles both of modernism and of its critique are simply too important to be abandoned as an invigorating, dynamic basis for thinking about the future of the city.

Here is a brief agenda for an urbanism both precedented and freely imagined:

1. REINFORCE NEIGHBOURHOODS

The neighbourhood must be at the centre. If the city is to resist the homogenisations of the global culture and to nurture local culture and participation, then the delineability and vigour of the neighbourhood must be assured. The neighbourhood is the means by which the social city is comprehended. Urban designers should work to create and reinforce neighbourhoods that situate both the conveniences and necessities of daily life within easy walking compass of places of residence, that maximise economic, social, cultural, and ecological self-sufficiency, that assert an autonomous physical character, and that share equitably in the benefits and responsibilities of the larger metropolis. Extent – the coalescence of scale, density, dimension, and activity – is the threshold of urbanity and we have lost the knack of its most intimate meanings.

2. MAKE IT SUSTAINABLE

The logic of urban ecology demands a restoration of the greatest reasonable degree of self-sufficiency: local self-reliance is the lesson of global interdependence. Urban designers must become the economists of energy cycles, oxygen production, thermal regulation, agriculture, raw and reused materials – all the quiddities of the city. The issue is not invariably to begin with a fixed form and imagine how it might be improved by modest variations – a catalytic converter, an airbag... – but to responsibly conjure the marvellous.

3. ADD GREEN EVERYWHERE

The city exists as both an exception and a complement to its territory, legible only in relation to the green spaces in which it sits and which sit in it. Use of these spaces is a fundamental right of city citizens and urban design should work to guarantee this in terms of convenience and variety, both private and public. This distribution of green should effect both the location of construction and its form. Consider, for example, the architecture that might result if the equivalent of fifty or seventy or a hundred percent of the surface of a city were to be green, how building might harbour and support it. We are too caught up in an artificial dichotomy between the city and nature: the house and garden (even the city and its parks) are only the most tentative and preliminary expressions of the possibilities.

4. SECURE THE EDGE
Cities run the risk of asphyxiating in their own extent. There is a boundary of apraxia, a point of absolute dysfunction beyond which the city simply can no longer perform coordinated actions. The urban edge secures the viability of the city both functionally and perceptually. The delineability of the city is pre-condition for a sense of citizenship, therefore of urban democracy. Again, the logic of governance in a globalising culture and economy will demand a strengthening of locality, not a progressive dissipation of the autonomy of cities into the increasingly artificial economies of nation-states. City edges – however permeable – are also formal, sets of places. It seems fundamental that one should be able to actually leave town: the 'edge city' means you never can.

5. MAKE PUBLIC PLACES
There is simply no substitute for the physical spaces of public assembly. Increasingly imperilled by commercialisation, electronification, criminality, and neglect, both the idea and the forms of gathering are a central subject for the imagination of urban design. Public space is the lever by which urban design works on the city, by which the subtle relations of public and private are nourished. A fixation on the media of production of these spaces has overcome any passion for their quality, even as a Nielsenesque resignation stupidly celebrates any gathering, however it is induced. Urban design must keep Giants' Stadium from annihilating Washington Square even as it seeks all the alternatives in-between. The Internet is great but it ain't Piazza Navona: free association and chance encounter still demand the meeting of bodies in space. Embodiment is the condition of accident and accident is a motor of democracy.

6. BE SURE ROOMS HAVE VIEWS
Modernist urbanism was not all bad. Le Corbusier's three qualities – light, air, and greenery – still form a matrix for urban design. The issue lies in making sure all the views are not the same. The architecture of the city is the compact of conflicting desires, continuously unfolding. If the American frontier offered a vision of absolute vision, of an untrammelled homestead unlimited by the physical presence of one's neighbour (a fantasy stoked by the sure psychical symmetry of Jefferson's infinite grid), the city is the instrument and the laboratory of adjudicated desire, in which every

happy inhabitation is the marker of agreement. Here is a site for thinking architecture, for a science and art of replacing rival, hostile, claims with a crafting of unvalenced difference. What is wanted is a city with an infinity of views that embody a luxury of choices, not a system of privileges.

7. FINESSE THE MIX

What has begun to happen to the city as locationality really begins to float is a saturation of the mix. As production ceases to foul the environment, as classes, races, and nationalities learn to desist in denying each others' enjoyment – enforcing segregation – and as communication becomes truly transparent, anything might appear anywhere. All the new species produced by our dizzyingly splicing culture demand a city in which they will be able to live together comfortably, not the zoning and monofunction of the planners. Urban design must keep pace by exploring the tectonics not simply of new use but of unpredictable transformation, creating cities that are as malleable as lofts and as fixed as works of art. One of the main territories of this investigation will necessarily be the compatibility of sizes, likely to become the main problematic of use harmonisation. Another will be the constant consideration of the appropriateness of various juxtapositions, questions of the deepest political and artistic import. Cities, after all, are juxtaposition engines, mutation machines. Theories of propriety, though, are necessary if we are to choose among endless possibilities and make the urban work collective.

8. ELABORATE MOVEMENT

It is time for a radical shift towards human locomotion in cities. The automobile is not simply a doomed technology in its current form, it has proved fundamentally inimical to urban density. Enforcing the hydra of attenuation and congestion, the car usurps the spaces of production and health, of circulation and enjoyment, of greenery, of safety. Fitted to the bodies of cities which could never have anticipated it, the car is a disaster in town. We cannot again repeat the mistake of retrofitting the city with a technology that does not love it, with railway cutting or freeways. Cars must lose their priority, yielding both to the absolute privilege of pedestrians and to something else as well, something that cannot yet be described, to a skein of movement each city contours to itself. This may well involve various forms of mechanical (or biological) technology but urban design – in considering the matter – should reject the mentality of available choices and formulate rational bases for fresh desires. If we cannot even describe the characteristics of superb urban transport – invisible? silent? small? leisurely? mobile in three axes? friendly? – this is because we have not taken the trouble to really imagine it.

9. LOCALISE ARCHITECTURE

Architecture is urban by convention, recording accumulated compacts. Climax is the key: cities are form-makers and urban design should astutely recognise indigenous forms that have reached some kind of perfection. Beautiful logics once established – whether the brownstones of Brooklyn or the labyrinths of Fex — are entitled to architectural citizenship, to a certain inalienability of rights. Climax — a term borrowed from foresters — is a condition of homeostasis, a permanent stage of growth. In cities, this must be nurtured both in use and in form. Form, after all, does enjoy a certain autonomy, originating in use and circumstances but eventually free of them. Reinforcing such character is a great task for urban design. Reproducing or simulating it is not. Fresh climaxes will not reproduce those of the past but will seek out new forms of locality. This new indigenous could come from anywhere in global culture, from the creativity of any individual, from bio-regional particulars or simply from memory. Urban design must cultivate the shoots of distinction.

10. DEFEND PRIVACY

We have probably spent a little too much time critiquing the failures of the public realm and not enough searching for alternatives to the dispirited lexicon of official public space and activity. Public space should be about choice and choice, finally, is a private matter. Public space needs to be rethought not simply as a series of sites but as a conceptual resource out of which an infinity of private fantasies and behaviours can be drawn, a construct at once ineffable and available, a vast collective reservoir for the watering of individual activities not yet imagined and possibly secret. The range of private choices which surround the public realm define it absolutely. Urban design is a bridge between these realms.

11. MAKE IT BEAUTIFUL

For urban *designers*, finally, there is no other goal. We are negligent in our tasks if we fail to engage deep desire, the means by which we enlarge the city of sense, the millionfold techniques of an urban erotics.

For projects by Michael Sorkin, the reader is referred to pls. 148-153.

The Technology of Perfection

RODO TISNADO

ARCHITECTURE AND TECHNOLOGY

Talking about architecture and technology as though they were two different things is almost a self-contradiction. Architecture is necessarily technological. When architecture uses technology it gives meaning to it. It is the work of the architect to give meaning to a building. That meaning is the transition of a building towards a work of architecture, a piece of the city.

THE CITY AND ARCHITECTURE

The city is a social invention of the 'human beast'. Human beings are fragile animals who need to mature slowly. After millions of years of slow Darwinian evolution, a Chinese person still needs twenty years to master his own language.

Fortunately about ten thousand years ago, the human animal invented the city, a place where he could find protection: outside the city there was no security. In French, in the word *ville* (city) there is the word *vie* (life).

The city is not the invention of one man, it is society as a whole that invented the city and gives it its directions for development. The city also cannot be the invention of an architect. Societies make cities but they give architects the possibility to make them evolve. By creating buildings and their environment, architects create the visible part of the city. The rest is a fact of society.

Architecture-Studio prefers to work in cities. Our means and our reasoning are more obviously useful in a context that is rich in history than out in the countryside. The city is the domain of the urban, which is forcibly artificial. In the city there is life, but artificial life. A tree is no longer a tree. Are there cats in the countryside?

TECHNOLOGICAL SPACE

There are several ways to create technological architecture. In another time, architects used a method which consisted in rendering visible the technical 'guts' of a building. We are more inclined to create technological space where the technology is invisible.

In 1981 when President Mitterrand launched his *grands projets* in Paris it was to enrich the city. We were fortunate enough to win the competition for the Arab World Institute (IMA) with Jean Nouvel (pls. 162, 163). It is because of this building that we came into contact with the Aga Khan Award in the late 1980s.

The IMA, an association of France with Arab countries, was intended as a kind of showroom of French technology in the presence of the new wealth of the Arab world – oil, an old, well-known product which had not until then been very expensive. Our response to this commission had to be up to the cultural importance given to the project in France and elsewhere. It was necessary to express the wealth of the Arab architectural heritage in a technological space. The geometric design of the protective diaphragms of the southern façade of the building was inspired by the geometric decomposition of the wall decoration of Arabic-Andalusian palaces in Spain. The spiral at IMA that receives books in the library is a transcription of the Tower of Samarra in Iraq.

We have engaged in transcribing 'signs' from Arab culture without ever giving way to the servile imitation of bad historicist architecture, which always imitates for the wrong reasons. The use of these signs was surely necessary opposite a jury entirely composed of personalities from the Arab world. The beauty of this technological poetry used in a functional context received the 1987 Aga Khan Award.

The technological 'calligraphy' of the diaphragms explained the calligraphy of the Arab book to the French. Though they cannot read these signs they are rendered intelligible by the diaphragms. In the same manner the silhouette of Paris re-transcribed through the north façade reconciles the Arab art object with its French setting.

MAGICAL TECHNOLOGY

A few years ago we participated in a competition to design the High School of the Future (pls. 160, 161). It was necessary to imagine a high school specialised in communication located near the Futuroscope in Poitiers. For Architecture-Studio all architecture must be in harmony with the culture of its time. The architecture of the past is easy to reproduce. It exists in any library. The architecture of the future does not exist yet and as such is impossible to represent. All that is left is the architecture of the present, the most difficult of all. Thus we imagined the future of the present. The resultant image makes reference to a spaceship. We gave it a fourth dimension, that of moment in a given time frame; a large disk moves along the main axis of the built triangle. The day of the high school begins at the moment when the disk begins its long voyage between the courtyard and its endpoint where it protects the students' restaurant, which we imagined as the cockpit of the spaceship. A simple technological system permits the disk to travel through space, creating, in what is already a magical architecture, a world of amazement that will motivate students to study the subjects of the visual future.

PRACTISING TECHNOLOGY

The city of Dunkirk decided to transform its old mercantile port into the headquarters of a new Coastal University. After a competition, the city asked us to transform the old tobacco warehouses into a Faculty of Climatic Engineering. We made use of the existing structure having emptied it of its floors. The empty shell became a leisure space for the faculty, and a location for local celebrations. We also made use of the existing street adding a new crossing point. We then covered the whole with a 'wave' made of aluminium. The nearby waves of the sea were thus metaphorically continued into the structure itself. Former port workers can still walk through this space that has been converted into classrooms where their children prepare for the professions of the future. The transition is thus made between the old port, with its dying traditional activities, its workers and the new school with its students. Technology here makes use of the poetry of the place... poetry about technology.

THE TECHNOLOGY OF TRANSPARENCY

The European Parliament in Strasbourg is the largest project ever carried out by Architecture-Studio (pls. 156, 157). This is the vessel of democracy. But there can be no democracy without institutional transparency. The chambers must be able to receive seven hundred parliamentarians. Because it is necessary to be able to transmit television images directly from the chambers, it was necessary to completely enclose the space. And yet democracy implies great transparency. The elliptical wooden volume of the chambers is integrated into the main structure opposite the water. A transparent façade forty metres high reveals the intensity of parliamentary debate through a fibre-optic system integrated into the wooden shell. Technology and transparency are the guarantee of democracy.

THE TECHNOLOGY OF PERFECTION

It took twelve years to build a small church in Paris in an area blighted by the urban experiments of the modern era, an area at the limits of the urban zone (pls. 158, 159). We protected the sacred space in a perfect wooden cube, "L'Arche d'alliance", made of a web of stainless steel as perfect as possible. This web serves at once as a link to the urban space and creates the necessary distance between the functions of the church and the city. The believer moves from his daily fragmented space to the sacred space. The interior is also made of wood, measured by the technology of perfection.

THE TECHNOLOGY OF MATERIALS

The Law Courts of Caen resemble an aggressive vessel born of a plan to renovate the urban core. A person who comes here to receive justice is necessarily intimidated. The image of justice is not smooth and homogenous but composite. It interrogates by its very presence. By way of contrast we have designed the interiors with humanity and softness in mind. The visitor enters the main hall with its overhead lighting and is immediately drawn towards the entrance to the courtrooms each of which is designed with different materials. Copper, wood, marble and cloth become symbolic of the various jurisdictions represented in the Law Courts. The interior of each courtroom is identical symbolising the fact that justice must be the same for all. The lighting is natural but indirect. This is a technology of materials used in the service of equality.

THE TECHNOLOGICAL SPACE FOR TECHNOLOGY
In a so-called *ville nouvelle* we created a technical high school (pls. 154, 155). A technical high school is intended to offer students the usual curriculum as well as specific training to prepare them for a profession. The high school is laid out according to the urban axes of the city. Along the straight road we created a 'classical' building for the general curriculum and along a curved road we designed a second structure for laboratories and technical training – the whole is enveloped in an aluminium skin based on industrial models. This is a reuse of a manufactured product in the service of a technological space for technology.

For projects by Rodo Tisnado/Architecture-Studio, the reader is referred to pls. 154-163.

Epilogue

BABAR KHAN MUMTAZ

This has been a rich discussion and presentation of what amounts to a broad survey of architecture, with an emphasis on the Islamic world, and especially Iran. There have also been presentations of significant architectural developments elsewhere in the world.

Though a number of issues have been raised, and a variety of technical and theoretical subjects discussed, all of these have a common theme that has formed a backdrop, tying them one to another by providing a context. Each of the presentations and sessions have, in effect, dealt with different ways of addressing the same question: how do we define the kind of architecture we want? How do we determine where we are and where we are, or should be, going?

Charles Jencks summarised this in a provocative manner in his presentation by asking, or rather asserting, that we are at a point of "paradigm shift". Where does an architectural paradigm come from? What brings it about? Firstly, it is the quality of architectural practice, thought and discourse that gives the architecture a direction, a structure. The coherence and the quality of architecture in a country or in a region at any given time is a function of, and determined by, the main forces that give it shape and direction – architectural education, professional bodies, building and development control, legislation, and of course, the clients.

Nader Ardalan spoke of the role of clients, and the public at large, in stimulating architectural response. The more debate, discussion and dialogue there is between those concerned, the better architecture will become. Secondly, the architectural paradigm is strengthened or weakened by the actions of those involved in architecture. Each time we are involved in architecture, whatever the context, we have to make a decision that influences the paradigm – not just locally, but perhaps globally, if we accept the interconnectedness of the 'butterfly effect'. The architect has to steer a course between a number of options. Like sailors, he can either remain in the shipping lanes, or use a compass to guide himself through uncharted waters. Such a course may prove profitable and exciting, or dangerous and difficult. However, instead of the pull of the magnetic field, architects are guided by four tensions that act simultaneously. These are:
- the tension between local and global factors – are architects responding to and desiring to be judged by local values, cultures and needs, or do they ignore these, and seek to emulate the best architects, and look to them for recognition and respect?

- the tension between conventional technologies and traditional materials, and cutting edge technologies and materials;
- the tension between architecture and the other arts and sciences. Should we form our notions of nature and the way it works by borrowing metaphors from the other disciplines? Charles Jencks suggests that unless architects want to appear antediluvian, they must revamp their view of the universe;
- the tension between standing out and blending in – should buildings acknowledge and respond to those that surround them? The ultimate blending in might be considered the glazed façades that have no form of their own and literally reflect their surroundings; or should architects deliberately make a statement? Ken Yeang responds that if you were designing in Beijing's Forbidden City, you certainly would not want it to stand out. On the other hand, Jencks showed us the work of architects that very definitely make a contribution to shifting the architectural paradigm.

These are not tensions that need to, or can, be resolved in a once and for all manner. Nor would the resolution of one tension automatically restrict the options in the others. Thus it is possible to design for a global audience using traditional materials in a way that stands out from its surroundings, and in a way that responds to the 'Jumping Universe'. The art is in how to resolve these in a responsible yet outstanding way. It is the many decisions being made by designers that come together in what one may call 'similar difference' that produces a paradigm.

Charles Jencks has said that he discerns the coming together of these similar differences in a discernable direction, leading to a paradigm shift. If we observe the very pluralistic nature of society, however, unless we take a very ethno-centric view of our world, what we have is actually a 'paradigm drift'.

Finally, to bring about paradigm shift, or even paradigm drift, we need to circulate information about new ideas and directions. Often in the other arts there is an avant-garde, an often illicit, underground movement – an art-house film or non-commercial trend that explores new ideas. What is the equivalent in architecture if we cannot put up a building? The equivalent is the project, which can be produced without a client and in defiance of regulations and restrictions if need be.

The Modern Movement owes much to the architectural project, especially by young, then-unknown architects, and that tradition has continued with Archigram or Zaha Hadid for example. How can we encourage the dissemination of the requisite knowledge of projects that might be required for an actual paradigm shift to occur? Here, as in other fields, the use of computers and the Internet is proving to be a boon: not only is it easier to produce a more convincing project, it is becoming much easier to pass work around. The ArchNet programme provides a platform and an opportunity to do this, but we also need to find other ways for young architects to explore alternatives and influence future paradigms.

Akram Abu Hamdan said that the vision of Charles Jencks is elitist because he uses the architecture of 'superstars' to prove his points. While these are wonderful buildings, they are all self-expressive and perhaps even self-indulgent. It is thus difficult to label them under a single banner, such as that of a paradigm shift. The point that Akram Abu Hamdan wanted to raise was whether there is room for such self-expression. He asked whether we are collectively trying to break out of the conventional, out of the confines or discipline of the grid. Is it, as Jencks says, that we are trying to simulate nature? The question that needs to be asked is, rather, why are we doing that? And even if we are, why are we using such precision computer-based technologies and such very complex tools to turn regular shapes into complex shapes? Nature evolved without recourse to such complexity, so to what extent can architects really use these complex technologies to imitate nature? Is this being sincere or is it merely a superficial diversion?

Akram Abu Hamdan went on to say that in Ardalan's work the ideas presented are very appealing, but is the client really the great patron, the driving force behind architectural excellence? Abu Hamdan's experience was that clients mostly do not know what they are talking about. For him the question was, more often than not: should I educate the client or obediently give form to their desires by delivering what they want or have described? For example, if the client wants something modern, should he give them a modern building or one based on traditional architecture?

Ali Saremi said that he recalled the time when Charles Jencks was talking about another paradigm shift in architecture, the one he famously called Post-Modernism. In 1974 during probably the last major seminar in Tehran, with the participation of Louis Kahn, James Stirling, Denise Scott-Brown, there was discussion of the paradigm shift towards Post-Modern architecture. Comparing that period to this one, it might be said that there were some similarities. Between architecture, and architectural education, there was to some extent, a consensus. But now the times have changed so much, there is a pluralism of styles and opinions, so that what is right and wrong, or good and bad in architecture, cannot readily be decided. There is a broad range of work and ideas, and that makes it very difficult to find agreement.

Darab Diba said that there is a need to focus on social, human oriented architecture. The question for modern architecture is how can we, through architecture, provide the basic conditions for people in need and those living in atrocious social conditions? He found it difficult to reconcile grandiose and opulent architecture, such as that of the Bilbao Guggenheim by Frank Gehry, with the very poor conditions under which so many people are living around the world. To him this was marginal architecture as far as the real world was concerned. He said that that morning there had been long sessions of the Juries for the main building of the Iranian Ministry of Oil. Substantially different projects were presented in the competition, and there were many different identities, cultures, contexts and technologies involved. Jencks would be pleased to know that there was even a 'Blob'!

In contrast, in 1962 there was Louis Kahn's winning project for the National Assembly in Dacca that was both appropriate and responsive. In thinking about good architecture, especially monuments and competition projects, good architecture is needed; whether socially oriented or an act of self-expression, both are needed. For example, Hassan Fathy was a modest person, working with the people of Gourna in Egypt, but what he produced was another approach to architecture. We cannot restrict ourselves to a single definition of the appropriate path for architecture.

Should they have to choose between one or the other type of architect, between a self-expressive designer or a social architect, or should both be considered legitimate? Darab Diba responded that life imposes its own challenges, and we respond to them. That is human nature, and to respond to something larger than oneself, one must give something. This idea of receiving and giving is the process of gaining acceptance. It also leads to my idea of being responsible as an architect. We need to be both self-expressive and socially responsible.

The Aga Khan Award has done a noble task, but it has focused almost exclusively on social need. When one comes to Tehran or Kuwait City or anywhere else in the Islamic world, the Award does not give the prominence required to major landmarks in those cities: the airports, shopping centres, office blocks, the form-giving projects. The Award has opted out of these form-giving projects. While recognising good architecture, the Award must also give direction. What Jencks calls "cosmogenesis" as an opening of the mind: reality is not a factory working on auto-pilot, it needs nurturing. It is a pity that in the Islamic world we have to receive our ideas of form from the likes of Norman Foster. The Award should not only concentrate on small projects and everyday architecture, but also on the major, formal building types.

Akram Abu Hamdan asked if there is no good and no bad in architecture; does that mean that anything goes? Diba responded that you try to do "your own thing" and to accept the views of others. The 'high-tech' approach of Norman Foster is contributing to civilisation, and so also is an architect working at the opposite end of the spectrum. We cannot categorise architecture into good or bad.

Jencks refers to the question of functional right or wrong that still gives architecture its value, but this question has become very hard to judge. Pluralism makes criticism very difficult, let alone saying what is right or wrong. Even in painting, there is a vast variety of styles, and they have the same problems. The real paradigm of this century is to find your own broad way between right and wrong.

Should we be accepting of all architecture, or should it be aiming at some particular objectives? If so, we need to state why, how, and what those objectives are. Perhaps the need for openness is more important than setting absolute standards. A respondent in the audience said that there have been long and fruitless discussions in Iran aimed at trying to understand culture and cultural issues. "We Iranians," he said, "don't need stagnation, we need to deal with global issues, and we need to open the country to new ways of expressing architecture." He went on to say that "Jencks' case is entirely about image – that is not what good or bad architecture is about. It is about experience, the planet and the human race. It is absolutely insane to use nature to judge architecture. Nature is entirely indifferent to us, it is up to us to respond and relate to nature."

Another respondent from the floor said that an important question for architects is how to look at nature and how to deal with nature. If the paradigm shift seems to be a logical result of the mechanistic view, then the paradigm we should be looking for is something in opposition to this scientific determinism. We need to look for some freedom of expression, to relate to the scale and needs of humans, and of urban society. Some architects, like Frank Gehry, have tried to create models of sculpture, while others, such as Norman Foster, have used science. By doing this we are getting closer to such a paradigm. This is something that has already been lost in the modern movement. The basis of the discussion should be: how far can we get back to the base of nature and closer to nature?

A commentator mentioned that Karl Popper in his *Open Society* said that the future is unknown and unknowable: in other words, if someone knows what will happen, they could prevent it; therefore it might not or could not happen. Thus we cannot suggest any form for future architecture, but only for contemporary architecture, for our own times, not for the future.

Another contributor to the debate noted that architecture is about experiences, of things, and of people. These are the underlying issues. When Jencks speaks of different traditions, we are being unkind if we say we are only looking at the images, since there are underlying issues that go along with them. We should see the image with the concept and idea behind it. We need to look at both together, and if we can try to do that, then we can see architecture in a more positive way.

The issues raised were not simple, and cannot be resolved easily, let alone in the context of a single seminar. However, the first step to the resolution of some of the questions is to open dialogue and debate.

For photographs of the seminar sessions, the reader is referred to pls. 164-170.

III.

II2.

II3.

110. Charles Jencks, Universe Cascade, Portrack, Scotland, Great Britain, 2001.

111. Santiago Calatrava, City of Arts and Sciences, Valencia, Spain, 1991-2002.

112. Frank Gehry, Guggenheim Bilbao, Bilbao, Spain, 1993-1997.

113. "Metaphors" of the Guggenheim Bilbao, Bilbao, Spain, 1993-1997.

114.

114. FOA (Moussavi and Zaero-Polo),
Yokohama International Port Terminal,
Japan, 1995-2002.

115. Norman Foster, Swiss Re Headquarters,
London, Great Britain, 1996-2002.

116. MvRdV, Dutch Pavilion, Expo 2000,
Hanover, Germany, 2000.

117. Daniel Libeskind, Imperial War
Museum-North, Manchester, Great Britain,
1998-2002.

115.   116.

117.

118.

119.

118, 119. Arata Isozaki, Isozaki Atea, Bilbao, Spain, 2001.

120. Antonio Sant'Elia, "Station for Aeroplanes and Trains with Funicular Railways and Elevators Connecting Three Street Levels", 1914, ink and pencil on paper, Musei Civici, Como, Italy.

121. Arata Isozaki, new Florence Station competition scheme, Florence, Italy, 2002.

122, 123. Arata Isozaki, new exit for the Uffizi Museum, competition scheme for Piazza Castellani, Florence, Italy, 1998.

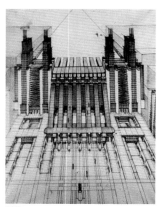

120.

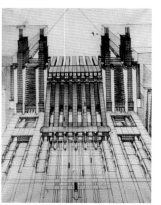

121.

122.

123.

124.

125.

126.

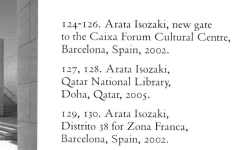

124-126. Arata Isozaki, new gate
to the Caixa Forum Cultural Centre,
Barcelona, Spain, 2002.

127, 128. Arata Isozaki,
Qatar National Library,
Doha, Qatar, 2005.

129, 130. Arata Isozaki,
Distrito 38 for Zona Franca,
Barcelona, Spain, 2002.

127.

129.

130.

131.

132.

133.

131. Frank Gehry, Experience Music Project, Seattle, Washington, United States, 1995-2000.

132. MvRdV, Metacity/Datatown, 1998.

133. Tadao Ando, Awaji Yumebutai, Awajishima, Hyogo, Japan, 1992-2003.

134.

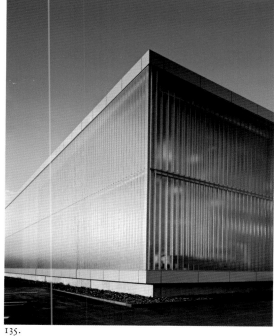

135.

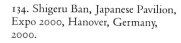

134. Shigeru Ban, Japanese Pavilion, Expo 2000, Hanover, Germany, 2000.

135. Wiel Arets, Lensvelt Factory and Offices, Breda, Netherlands, 1995-2000.

136, 137. Asymptote, Virtual Guggenheim Museum, 1999-2002.

138. Yoshio Taniguchi, Gallery of Horyuji Treasures, Tokyo National Museum, Tokyo, Japan, 1994-1999.

139. Alvaro Siza, Serralves Foundation, Porto, Portugal, 1991-1999.

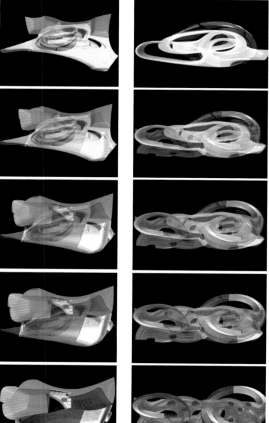

136.   137.

138.

139.

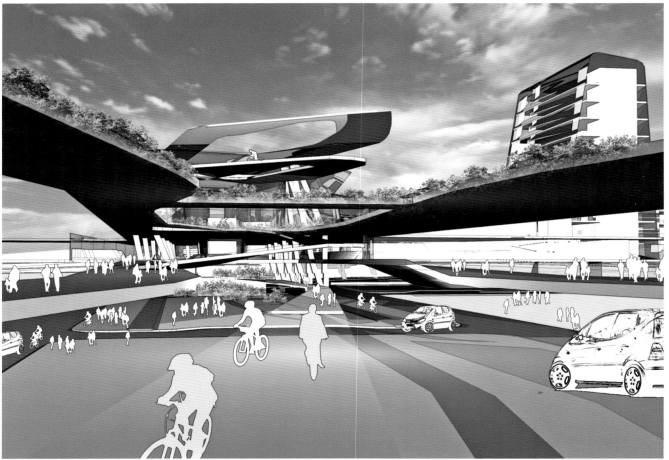

140.

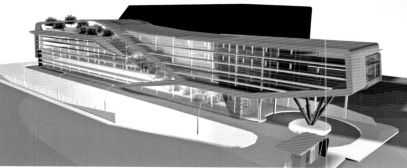

142.

143.

144.

140. Ken Yeang, Amsterdam Centre of Science and Technology, entrance, Watergraafsmeer, Amsterdam, Netherlands, 1998.

141. Ken Yeang, Amsterdam Centre of Science and Technology, aerial view, Watergraafsmeer, Amsterdam, Netherlands, 1998.

142. Ken Yeang, Mewah Oils Headquarters, Pulau Indah Industrial Park, Port Klang (Westport), Selangor, Malaysia, 2001-2003.

143, 144. Ken Yeang, Menara Umno, Jalan Macalister, Penang, Malaysia, 1998.

145.

146.

145-147. Ken Yeang, Parramata Road, Sydney, Australia, 2000.

147.

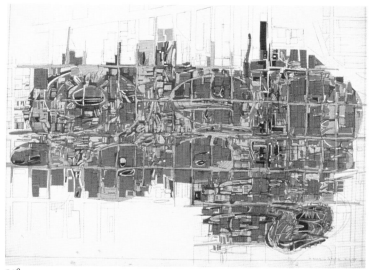

149.

150.

151.

148, 149. Michael Sorkin, East New York Community
Masterplan, Brooklyn, New York, NY, United States, 1995.

150, 151. Michael Sorkin, House of the Future,
imaginary site somewhere in the United States, 1999.

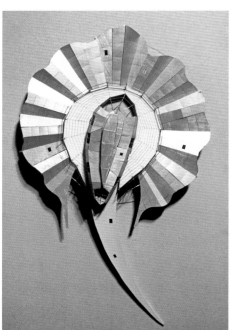

152.

153.

152. Michael Sorkin, Ray, one of a series of Beached Houses designed for a site in White House, Jamaica, 1989.

153. Michael Sorkin, Weed, Arizona, model of a proposed new town on the Colorado River near Yuma, United States, 1994.

154.

155.

156.

157.

154, 155. Architecture-Studio, Jules Verne High School, Cergy-Le-Haut, France, 1991-1993.

156, 157. Architecture-Studio (Martin Robain, Rodo Tisnado, Jean-François Bonne, A. Bretagnolle, R. H. Arnaud, L. M. Fischer, M. Lehmann, R. Ayache) and G. Valente, European Parliament, Strasbourg, France, 1991-1998.

158.

159.

160.

161.

158, 159. Architecture-Studio, Our Lady of the Ark
of the Covenant Church, Paris, France, 1986-1998.

160, 161. Architecture-Studio (Martin Robain,
Rodo Tisnado, Jean-François Bonne, Jean-François
Galmiche) and F. X. Désert, High School
of the Future, Jaunay-Clan, France, 1987.

162.

162, 163. Architecture-Studio
(Martin Robain, Rodo Tisnado,
Jean-François Bonne, Jean-François Galmiche)
and Jean Nouvel, G. Lezenes and P. Soria,
Arab World Institute, Paris, France, 1981-1987.

163.

164.

165.

166.

167.

164. Participants in Yazd.

165. Ali Reza Sami Azar.

166. Pirooz Hanachi.

167. Seyyed Mohammad Beheshti.

168.

169.

168. A crowd, consisting in good part of students, awaits entry to a seminar session in the Tehran Museum of Contemporary Art.

169. Front row in the Tehran Museum of Contemporary Art. From left to right, Nassim Sharipov, Charles Jencks, Ali Reza Sami Azar, Sémia Akrout-Yaïche, Selma al-Radi and Suha Özkan.

170. Sessions in the Tehran Museum of Contemporary Art.

170.

Appendix
LIST OF PARTICIPANTS

AKRAM ABU HAMDAN
Architect, Director General of the National Resources Investment and Development Corporation for the Revitalisation of Amman, Jordan.

SÉMIA AKROUT-YAÏCHE
Architect, Director of the Association for Safeguarding the Medina, the rehabilitation office for the old city of Tunis, Tunisia.

NOOREDDIN ALLAHDINI
Researcher, Institute of Ismaili Studies, London, United Kingdom.

SELMA AL-RADI
Archaeologist, international expert on restoration, advisor to the National Museum of Sana'a, restorer of the 'Amiriya Madrasa in Rada', Yemen.

NADER ARDALAN
Architect, senior partner in KEO Consulting, Kuwait.

BAGHER AYATOLLAHZADEH SHIRAZI
Architect and conservation specialist, head of the Iranian ICOMOS, Tehran, Iran.

AYDAN BALAMIR
Architect and educator, Faculty of Architecture, Middle East Technical University, Ankara, Turkey.

SEYYED MOHAMMAD BEHESHTI
Vice Minister of Culture and Head of the Iranian Cultural Heritage Organisation, Tehran, Iran.

STEFANO BIANCA
Director of the Historic Cities Support Programme, Aga Khan Trust for Culture, Geneva, Switzerland.

PETER DAVEY
Editor, *Architectural Review*, London, United Kingdom.

FARROKH DERAKHSHANI
Director of Award Procedures, Aga Khan Award for Architecture, Geneva, Switzerland.

DARAB DIBA
Architect and educator, Faculty of Fine Arts, Tehran University, Iran.

IRAJ ETESSAM
Architect and educator, Faculty of Fine Arts, Tehran University, Iran.

PIROOZ HANACHI
Vice Minister of Housing and Urban Development, Tehran, Iran.

HASHEM HASHEM NEJAD
Architect and educator, Faculty of Architecture, University of Science and Technology, Tehran, Iran.

RENATA HOLOD
Art and architectural historian, professor and chair of the Graduate School of the History of Art, University of Pennsylvania, United States.

ARATA ISOZAKI
Architect, founding member of the Metabolist Group, Tokyo, Japan.

CHARLES JENCKS
American architectural historian and architect, author of *Post-Modern Architecture* and *The New Paradigm in Architecture*, London, United Kingdom.

PHILIP JODIDIO
Author on art and architecture, former editor of *Connaissance des Arts*; author of the recent book *Architecture Now!*, Paris, France, and United States.

OSSAMA KABBANI
Architect, director of the 'Solidère' initiative for the reconstruction of Beirut, Lebanon.

MOHAMMAD HASSAN KHADEMZADEH
Director of the Iranian Cultural Heritage Organisation of Yazd Province, Iran.

KAZEM MANDEGARI
Architect and educator, School of Architecture, Yazd, Iran.

S. HADI MIRMIRAN
Architect, Naqsh-e-Jahan Pars Consultants, Tehran, Iran.

LUÏS MONREAL
General Manager of the Aga Khan Trust for Culture, Geneva, Switzerland.

BABAR KHAN MUMTAZ
Architect and development expert, reader in Housing Studies,
University College, London, United Kingdom.

AZDINE NEKMOUCHE
Architect, president of the Order of Moroccan Architects,
Casablanca, Morocco.

SUHA ÖZKAN
Secretary General of the Aga Khan Award for Architecture,
Geneva, Switzerland.

ATTILIO PETRUCCIOLI
Architectural historian and educator, founder and director
of the Islamic Environmental Design Research Centre,
and professor at Bari Polytechnic Institute, Italy.

EDUARDO PORTA
Archaeologist and restoration expert, Barcelona, Spain.

ALI REZA SAMI AZAR
Director of the Tehran Museum of Contemporary Art, Tehran, Iran.

ALI SAREMI
Architect and educator, Tajeer Architectural Consultants, Tehran,
Iran.

NASSIM SHARIPOV
Architect and restoration expert, former chief architect of Bukhara,
Uzbekistan.

MICHAEL SORKIN
Architect, critic and author, frequent contributor to *Village Voice*
and *Architectural Record*, New York, NY, United States.

FARHAD TEHRANI
Architect and educator, Faculty of Architecture, Shahid Beheshti
University, Tehran, Iran.

RODO TISNADO
Architect, founding partner of the firm Architecture-Studio, Paris,
France.

SHADIA TOUQAN
Architect and restoration expert, director of the Technical Office
of the Old City of Jerusalem Revitalisation Programme, Jerusalem.

ABDOLRAHMAN VAHABZADEH
Economist and educator, Faculty of Architecture, Shahid Beheshti
University, Tehran, Iran.

KEN YEANG
Architect, proponent of bio-climatic architecture and urban form
in tropical environments, Kuala Lumpur, Malaysia.

Publication credits

Kamran Adle
M. Ahmadian
Mohamed Akram
Mokhless al-Hariri
Alain Photo
Tadao Ando
Architecture-Studio
Nader Ardalan
ASM
Asymptote
Bavand Consultants
Jacques Bétant
Stefano Bianca
Tim Bradley

Chamber of Architects, Ankara
Stéphane Couturier
Farrokh Derakhshani
Cemal Emden
Georges Fessy
FOA
Khaled Frikha
Gaston
Murat Germen
Reha Günay
Hamzah and Yeang
Tim Hursley
Anwar Hussain
ICHO, Yazd

Arata Isozaki
Charles Jencks
Merih Karaaslan
Pervez Khan
Toshiharu Kitajima
K.L.Ng
Saleh Lamei-Mostafa
METU Faculty of Architecture
Khadija Mhedhebi
S. Hadi Mirmiran
MvRdV
OCJRP
Robin Oldacre
Gary Otte

Suha Özkan
Christian Richters
Kamran Safamanesh
Sharestan Consultants
Sami Sisa
SOM
Michael Sorkin
Murat Tabanlıoğlu
Doğan Tekeli
TMCA
Fernando Urquijo
Madelon Vriesendorp
Ken Yeang
Necati Yurtsever

`

EDITORIAL COORDINATION PHILIP JODIDIO (FOR AKTC); HARRIET GRAHAM (FOR UMBERTO ALLEMANDI & C.)

COPY-EDITING HARRIET GRAHAM

LAYOUT ALESSANDRA BARRA

PHOTOLITHOGRAPHY FOTOMEC, TURIN, ITALY

PUBLISHED BY UMBERTO ALLEMANDI & C., TURIN, ITALY

PRINTED IN ITALY, OCTOBER 2004

ISBN 88-422-1236-9